THE SEX
OF THE
DOLLAR

STREET-SMART
FINANCIAL PLANNING
FOR WOMEN

BY

ANNE KOHN BLAU
with Ellen Thro

SIMON AND SCHUSTER

New York   London   Toronto   Sydney   Tokyo

Published by Simon and Schuster
A Division of Simon & Schuster, Inc.
Simon & Schuster Building
Rockefeller Center
1230 Avenue of the Americas
New York, New York 10020

SIMON AND SCHUSTER and colophon are registered trademarks
of Simon & Schuster, Inc.

Designed by Irving Perkins Associates
Manufactured in the United States of America

1   3   5   7   9   10   8   6   4   2

Library of Congress Cataloging in Publication Data

Blau, Anne Kohn.
The sex of dollar.

Includes index.
1. Women—United States—Finance, Personal.
I. Thro, Ellen.   II. Title.
HG181.B46   1988   332.024'042   87-23560
ISBN 0–671–60680–8

FOR MY MOTHER
who taught me by example to believe
that all things are possible;
and
FOR MY HUSBAND
supportive of all things I attempt.

═══CONTENTS═══

FOREWORD

When I was a child, I was very impressed by a Chinese story that went like this:

> A little rich girl lived in a mansion with many servants to take care of all her needs. One day misfortune came upon the family, and all the servants were sent away. She asked her mother, what was she to do now?
>
> The mother told the little girl that she shouldn't worry, because she would always have ten little servants, pointing to the girl's own ten little fingers.

This story affected my life. Later, when I was an adult woman unexpectedly on my own, I understood that, ultimately, our care is in our own hands. And I also learned I could take care of myself.

1

Women Insecurities

DIFFERENCES BETWEEN THE WAYS
WOMEN AND MEN DEAL WITH MONEY

WHEN I lived in Mississippi, I heard women refer to their "egg money," which I found out meant their discretionary funds, money they could spend any way they pleased. The phrase originated in the olden days in rural areas, where husband and wife worked equally hard, but all the money was controlled by the man who was the head of the household. There was, however, one exception: The wife was allowed to keep and manage the money she made from selling the eggs laid by the family's chickens. So if her chickens came home to roost, she could accumulate and control a small nest egg all her own.

Today, women have more funds to manage, but too many of us still act as if we were just handling the "extra" money. Even if the funds are central to our lives, we tend to think of it as "egg money."

In general, women relate to money differently than men do:

- Men value power; women value security.
- Men take risks; women are conservative.
- Men like action and take the initiative; women react and accept the consequences.
- Men like competition; women like accommodation.
- Men are eager to borrow; women would rather not.
- Men trade options and commodities; women buy bonds.
- Men like charts of market behavior; women like Louis Rukeyser on PBS's "Wall Street Week."
- Men think of stockbrokers as fellow businesspeople; women think of them as providers of personal services.
- Men think of their financial independence as natural and eternal; women think of it as a temporary and extraordinary event.

What are the reasons for these different attitudes toward security and risk, and toward money and the business of business?

Women have long been accustomed to avoiding financial matters, leaving that responsibility to men, the traditional breadwinners. Recently, though, more of us have been participating in financial decisions, as well as making the money. I have noticed an increased interest by women in learning about finance, but many of the women I have met who manage their own money admit they do so only when forced to. Why? Because they have no male protector. They don't necessarily want the job.

I can understand this attitude perfectly; I used to be the same way. Once a housewife in Mississippi, I have transformed myself from a dependent woman to one who is on her own with a successful career as an investment broker and financial consultant. As a divorced mother without career experience, the going was tough and frightening at first. Taking care of myself and my family, making my own decisions, taking risks, and living by the results of these decisions was a new way of life, not without some failures. But I found the challenge exciting and unexpectedly satisfying, and I gained confidence in my own abilities. I experimented with various jobs before I found my niche in sales—I enjoy being with people, talking to them, and understanding their business needs. I started by selling advertising "time" in broadcasting. I established my credentials at radio stations, then worked for a television station in the Miami area.

I began to understand a new reality, what the male-dominated, business/financial world was really about. It was a different world than the one I had perceived as a homemaker listening to business talk at the dinner table. I discovered that an ability to assess a situation, project possible results, and make a decision were what counted in the world of business, and that the most important characteristic for success was an attitude of self-reliance.

Always curious about the world of finance, and concerned with my own future financial security, I wanted to learn about money. My selling skills and enthusiasm provided the entree into a financial career.

In 1977, there were few women investment brokers. Far from intimidating me, it was a challenge. I started my training with Bache & Co. in San Diego, California, where I had moved with my children when I remarried. My self-reliance and need for independence (even within marriage) had become stubbornly established as part of my personality. Money was no longer a mystery, a male prerogative, and it was fascinating.

The attitudes women used to have toward finance—fear, lack of interest and understanding, and complacency—still prevail. Even today, women dress for success, but they don't understand the mind-set necessary in order to succeed. They do not plan their financial lives with the same care that they plan their wardrobes and work lives. Many women fail to realize that by not understanding the basics of finance, especially their own, or by giving up control to others, they are still making financial decisions. But this "deciding by not deciding" carries dangers for their present and future life.

The main danger is a continuing modern version of dependency. Few men have expectations of deserving protection and care. For the most part, women still do. This problem, which at one time I shared, is a vital issue for many women today, whatever their ages or their situations in life—single, married, divorced, widowed. Taking responsibility for yourself must include learning to take responsibility for your own finances.

ATTITUDE

Many of my clients exemplify today's modern woman. Though playing contemporary roles, they have remained uninformed in money matters, held back by their own inaction as well as by a lack of critical information—too many Miss Muffets, not enough dragon-slayers. Let me give you a couple of examples from my own experience.

A certain Ms. Muffet, mother of two, sued Spiderman for divorce after six years of marriage. His income was in six figures. She had past experience as a teacher and could earn about $25,000 a year. She asked for $2,500 a month for six years as alimony, plus total child support, the house, and half the value of his business. Since it was a community property state, she ended up with a net worth of $250,000 plus support. She feels she deserves a life-style that is unchanged.

Another divorced mother is an artist struggling in the artistic tradition who is having a hard time meeting daily expenses. She receives $500 a month for support of her five-year-old son, which is enough to pay the rent on her studio apartment, a converted warehouse. The father has promised to pay for the child's college education, so she is not worried about her son's future. As an artist, she considers money to be a mundane preoccupation of materialistic people. Dealing with finance interferes with her creative time. Yet she admits to tension about money since her living expenses are never certain and her income is sporadic. A supplementary job would not make her feel good. Her only thought about her future is the hope that her father will leave her a reasonable inheritance someday.

Both of these women consider themselves "liberated." They are, after all, living on their own. Yet both expect their material needs to be taken care of just like the traditional wife who asks her husband for spending money. Both acquired money through personal interactions with men, and with those men out of the picture, they are uncertain about how to manage their own assets, let alone plan for the future.

POWER AND MONEY

A male acquaintance, hearing I was writing a book, asked what the subject was. "Women and money," I said. He immediately retorted, "Oh, you mean love and power!"

"Not exactly," I said. I was not writing a book about money from a man's point of view and the goals of sex and power. I was writing the book for women, from a woman's perspective, and toward the goal of self-empowerment.

Men understand the implicit connection between money and power. That power, in fact, may be of more importance to them than the bills and the coins. Men in search of power are very competitive and risk-oriented. Power, control of others—whether political or personal—can be bought in modern society. Women have chosen not to recognize this fact. Without much thought, we have delegated the power to control our financial lives, and often our security, to men. Although we have sought and won power in the job market, sometimes at the cost of male relationships, we have for the most part not challenged the power of finance. Many of us have even neglected to gain control over our own security, and by "security" I mean having control over the assets necessary for a standard of living we wish to maintain or achieve and still have enough for other life goals. Some women never own independent money during much of their lifetimes. Others own it, but have no control over it.

Women, particularly in the Western world, have sought and achieved a great deal of equality in their lives. The feminist movement brought to the world the awareness of women's desire to participate more fully in careers, politics, and sports. We are more conscious of the language and behavior of equality. And for some of us, the traditional female duties of home and children are shared by our men. But in finance—the one area crucial to real freedom and control over our lives—men still dominate. Even the feminist movement, for the most part, has neglected this "mundane" issue. This is true on the personal level, and on the world economic level. There are not many powerful women making central financial decisions in government as national economic advisers or as ministers of finance; nor are many women shaping far-reaching financial policy in corporate business as CEOs. Men have not volunteered to give up this power, and apparently women have lacked the opportunity, confidence, or desire to take it away from them.

> *Peter, Peter, pumpkin eater,*
> *Had a wife but couldn't keep her.*
> *Put her in a pumpkin shell,*
> *And there he kept her very well.*

Mrs. Petunia Smart, age sixty-six, is attractive—strong, lean, with determined eyes and gray curls. It is difficult to keep up with her dynamic mental and physical pace. She is enlightened and sensitive. A precocious child, she had a college degree by age nineteen and earned a Ph.D. in biology. Now she is retired and, financially, she could be on her own.

Typically, Petunia's husband, Paul, managed all their affairs as a responsible husband. They had been separated for several years when she presented herself in my office. Petunia says that Paul has become irrational in his behavior. He has become a recluse and she never sees him. She says she still misses him.

Incredibly, Paul still manages all the money, most of which is *hers* from a family inheritance. Petunia, a capable woman with a mind of her own, successful in her career, says she was brought up not to think about dealing with money. She feels there are more important things for her to be involved with, and that money in itself is a little "dirty."

Put her in a pumpkin shell . . .

Is irrational Paul managing the money responsibly? Petunia doesn't know, and decides "not to worry about it."

My extensive experience in financial planning for clients of both sexes shows this attitude is true for successful career women of all ages as well as for the more traditional woman working at home. That, perhaps, is not so surprising, but it does surprise me that all too few younger women in successful professional careers are in control of their own finances.

COMPETITION

Competition is one of the major ways in which women and men differ in their approach to finance. As a very revealing and pertinent example, consider the following description of male behavior (which appeared in *The New York Times Magazine* late in 1984, in a feature entitled "About Men"). To paraphrase:

> A man in his late thirties states that when he walks down the street, he sizes up every man who walks toward him and decides whether or not he can take him physically. He says that he learned this as a little kid, and that he has ambivalent feelings about continuing to judge people this way. He does recognize that his ambivalence arises partly because he realizes more guys could take him than formerly, because he is getting older. He wonders about the suitability of this thinking, but is not yet ready to give it up.

This story provides significant insight into male behavior and motivation: The desire to compete and win relates directly to the "corporate culture" of most business organizations where "the winning attitude" is stressed and in which "success" means being the "winningest." That is the goal.

My guess is that a woman walking down the street will size up other women to determine who is the most beautiful—the "mirror, mirror on the wall" syndrome. We know good looks help to get a man, and we make comparisons. The difference between these two "street games" is that the man's leads to independence, the woman's to dependence.

We are certainly more aware today, in bringing up a new generation of females, of the need to encourage independence, to inspire them to widen their horizons. Yet our society, for the most part, still seems to fall short when it comes to encouraging them to prepare and assume *financial* control over their own lives, an essential ingredient for independence.

That is the goal of this book. And to achieve it, you first

have to examine your own attitudes toward self-reliance
and money. Then, on a practical basis, I will help you learn
how to:

- Deal with the business world
- Do your own financial planning in a simple, flexible, and
  dynamic way
- Cope with inflation and adjust to the effects of the new tax
  law
- Achieve a frame of reference for a wide spectrum of
  investments and their critical characteristics
- Make financial decisions that fit both your present circumstances and your future goals.

This may seem like a tall order. But, once you understand
the concepts, I think you will find it more logical and easier
than you expect. And as you read this book, I hope you will
keep in mind that if women demand equal treatment from
society, we must also learn to take responsibility for
ourselves.

CHAPTER

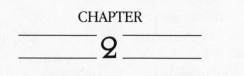

2

It's Only Money

COMMON SENSE ABOUT DOLLARS AND CENTS

ABOVE all, I am a practical person. So I am interested in money. I recognize that it is money which gives me the things I need and want, affords me certain experiences, and provides me with some of the security I require. As a practical person, I have always tried to deal with the world as it really is. I never thought that meat originated in the grocery store in little plastic packages. I knew how it got there. I do not believe it is the money itself that makes me happy, or that it is a valuable item to be collected. But I recognize its place in the practical world.

To understand what money is, remember its origin.

In the beginning there was the barter system: I offered you ten vats of olive oil for your load of flax for weaving. But ten vats of olive oil were clumsy to carry around, especially if you wanted to use them as you shopped. So "money" was invented, a portable object with a specific value on which everyone agreed. Money could be shells (remember wampum?), disks of silver, or rectangles of paper certified by the ruling authority.

Today, in the world of electronics, "money" is often blips in a computerized bookkeeping system. You can think of each blip as a gold star. If you have interest, Social Security, or a paycheck put into your checking account by "direct deposit," blips or "gold stars" are credited to it, not actual dollar bills. And if you use a plastic card in your banking machine to pay a utility bill or transfer money to another account, you are spending your "gold stars."

Before

Checking Account	Utility Company Account
****	—

After

Checking Account	Utility Company Account
***	*

This is how international foreign currency trades work. "Money" zooms around the world via computerized blips in a variety of financial transactions. Some day, gold stars in the form of computerized blips may replace coins, paper money, and checks altogether.

EARNINGS AND ASSETS

Whatever its form, money can also be differentiated by its source: earnings, which are money produced directly by work in the form of salary, fees, or commissions; and assets, which are various forms of property, including money itself, from which income can be derived.

A woman I admire built a very successful business through her own initiative and ideas. She came to my office requesting help in personal financial planning. She told me she was now worth $1 million, but that she was "cash poor"; she did not have enough income from the business for her personal use. She wanted to find a way to translate her net worth into the life-style that she felt she had earned. Her assets, though very real, were not benefiting her as she wished.

Many women are in this situation—high net worth yet inadequate income—because their assets—a home, paintings, jewelry, or antiques—do not produce any income, and may be difficult to sell should they so desire. Diamonds are not a "girl's best friend" when she needs money to pay her rent. Turning such assets into cash can be a tough decision, but financial planning techniques can help to determine when to convert assets to income and how much is appropriate in each situation.

Many young professional women have the opposite problem: high salaries but, after deductions and living expenses, little left for savings. Their assets are in the form of earnings, not investment potential. How to save the large lump sum needed to buy a house or start a business? This, too, is a job for financial planning, deciding the appropriate amount to save and how to invest those savings for the best results. It is savings, whether in the form of "leftovers" from earned income or appreciating business assets or in equity in your home, that provides the necessary ingredients for asset growth.

One woman I know lived modestly for many years without attempting to improve her situation in a well-paying career; instead, she waited for "potential assets" from the family trust. Her father had put the family assets into a lifetime trust for her mother, who lived to the age of ninety-four. When the daughter finally inherited—at age seventy—it was indeed a significant sum. Now, she thought, it was time for her to understand investing concepts and to live the life-style she had planned for so long. However, the "promise" of wealth that had sustained her also prevented her from accumulating her own asset base and enjoying herself in the prime of her life. This woman had neither adequate earnings nor assets during most of her life.

Is your income derived from earnings, assets, or some combination of both? The answer to that question is an important consideration in every financial plan. Most people over their lifetime have some of each. If you have mostly acquired assets and small earnings, your investment base is already set. If you have mostly earnings and few acquired assets, you need to build an investment base as you earn. If you can't easily replace your assets, it is usual to be more conservative and protective of them. On the other hand, if you have little to lose and have an ongoing stream of earnings, you might take more risks in building your investment base.

We tend to start life mostly with earnings and few assets. In our later years, our earning capacity may decrease, but we may be lucky enough to have sufficient assets to replace our wages. Some people rely solely on Social Security or pension income; others have additional assets from savings or inheritances that help determine their life-styles. All of these sources of income are important factors in your overall financial plan.

Age is also an important factor, not only in the probable source of your assets, but in the kind of investments you should choose as regards to risk level. Younger women are often optimistic, and with an ongoing income stream they may take on higher-risk, growth-oriented investments. Older investors, on the whole, may be more conservative because they are likely to have experienced financial loss somewhere in the past and recognize the need to preserve what they have. They cannot replace losses with new earnings. Typically:

	AGE 20–29	AGE 30–40	AGE 41–59	AGE 60–
Earned income	$	$$$	$$$$	$$
Investment assets	–	$	$$	$$$$
Investment strategy	Save	Risk & Growth	Growth & Risk	Conserve

These "typical" profiles of women's earnings, assets, and investment strategies throughout their lifetimes are presented more concretely in Chapter 11 in sample financial plans.

There is another interesting correlation to note about assets and earnings. In the past, it was generally men who made the earnings and women who inherited the assets. Today, that is not necessarily the case. Still, most insurance policies are on the husband's life, with the wife as beneficiary—reinforcing the concept that the man's salary is the predominant factor in most family earnings. It is a statistical fact that women earn less than men, but since women as a group tend to live longer than men, women end up with most of the assets.

I think there is a connection between aggressive earning power, the way men make their money, and risk. Women more often have "passive" income from asset management and invest for income rather than asset growth. It might follow, then, that women are more conservative and guarded with their money. In fact, that attitude may carry over to investment strategy generally, even when women become strong wage earners.

Note that I do not consider such conservatism on the part of women to always be a bad thing. At least some of men's investment risk-taking may be "war games," not true assertive investing. True conservatism in investment does not have to be either passive or unrewarding. Being conserva-

tive in a positive way requires two things: being aware of
our needs, and then planning how to get and keep what is
necessary to fulfill those needs. This is realism, unclouded
by lingering attitudes of dependency.

WHAT DOES MONEY MEAN TO YOU?

Money means different things to different people. If the rich
felt that they had enough of it, they would quit work and not
produce more. They would not invest what is called "risk
capital" in the hopes of increasing their assets dramatically.
Even the very rich can eat only so many croissants in one
day! But most of them cannot say how much money is
"enough."

The billionaire Hunt family was so worried about the
effect inflation would have on their money that during
the last decade they took significant investment risks in
silver, oil, sugar, and real estate. When one of the Hunt
brothers was asked about their losses in the silver market
($1 billion plus), he allegedly replied, "A billion dollars
isn't what it used to be." As it turned out, Mr. Hunt has had
a reversal of his fortune, and he could have used the extra
billion.

In our society, money is frequently a measure of success.
And success is competitive, a measurement with others in
the race to be on top. Money is also a measure of status and
power; it is how, in sports terminology, "you keep score."
Yet for many, what is more important than competition is to
have enough to achieve a desired way of life, what each of
us describes as *security*. Such security is closely linked to
that most emotional of qualities, our *self-esteem*.

This combination of power, security, and self-esteem
influences all the decisions we make about money. People
make emotional decisions about money because money
often represents more than the apparent transaction. Some

people scrimp and save because they feel they can't "afford" to do otherwise. Others spend lavishly with no real idea of whether they can afford it or not. I have noticed that the way people feel about money may be totally unrelated to the reality of their own situation.

Mrs. Z., a client of mine, was so concerned about how she should spend her money that she consulted me anxiously about the cost of replacing the family-room rug. Since this client was a real estate heiress with a significant income, she could easily afford to buy a very expensive rug, and it should hardly have been a matter of crisis. Her indecision was really an indication of her own feelings of dependency. Ms. A., another client, who could not easily afford it, had no such indecision about buying a new Mercedes and instructing me to liquidate a portion of her assets for this purpose. For her the car, not the money, fulfilled her emotional needs.

For Mrs. Z. it was security, for Ms. A. status, and both are legitimate emotional needs. Their decisions on spending, however, should be balanced with recognition of their longer-range financial planning requirements.

People talk about "having money" as if it were a defined, qualifying amount for belonging to a private club. If they "had it" they would be part of a charmed circle that didn't have to worry. Money would solve all their problems. The advertisements we see for owning goods and buying services, the life-style portrayed on some television shows, give many people unrealistic expectations. Lotteries and sweepstakes lure us with the same promises. Women and men alike, earning a high salary, who cannot save money, are often victims of their perceived "needs." Interestingly, people usually "raise the ante," or increase their financial needs proportionately, as their income goes up.

The terms *rich* and *poor* are, of course, relative, measured by the standards of our social group or by those passed on by our parents. However, the facts of rich and poor in this country, as they are defined by government standards, might surprise you. Some real numbers in the spectrum:

*Median income: Married $28,300
              Single women ⎫ with or without   11,800
              Single men   ⎭   dependent   15,500

Poverty line, family of four, Social Security Administration: $9,800

Source: U.S. Government Data, Current Population Reports, Consumer Income Series P60 #146, adjusted 1986.

You are probably richer than you thought!

In addition to family and social standards, how women feel about their money is often related to how they got it. Was it earned, inherited, married into, or divorced from? How long have they had it? Have they "always" had it, or have they known good times and bad, ups and downs? If they are accustomed to wealth, and it came easily, they may be more relaxed about money matters. Or, conversely, they may have "inherited" guilt about spending money from other family members. Some women with "old money," though secure in their status, can be very tight. For women who earned it "the hard way," money may become an ongoing preoccupation. The variations seem endless. Some women are very secretive about their finances; others brag and show off. Some pretend that concern about money is not genteel: It is somehow "dirty." To others, money is a burden or a bore: They don't want to spend their time on it.

The way you feel about money and the way you feel about yourself in relation to money are vital concerns in learning to control your own finances. The economical homemaker with only her "egg money" to spend and the family checkbook to balance belongs to the past. Yet too many women (let alone men) still think that money management is a male prerogative and duty. That idea alone is the most damaging to women and to their control over their lives. At worst, it is a form of exploitation; at best, it prevents women from controlling their own finances and planning and achieving their own financial goals.

If you intend to enter the financial world at all—and if you earn or control *any* money—you must do two things: You must learn about money, recognize your feelings about it and relate them to reality. And, of course, you must learn the rules of the game. Sports terminology is appropriate when discussing money, for the rules for sports and the rules of the financial world were both set down by men.

3

Play to Win

THE RULES OF THE MONEY GAME

DESPITE all its complex rules and variations, the money game is essentially very simple. It is the business of using money to make money. However, always keep in mind your purpose in making money—its use value—because there are different ways to make it, tied to different levels of risk. Regardless of what game you play, you can either win or lose, and in the investment game, there can be degrees of winning and losing. As a general rule, men are willing to take greater risks than women, in both their careers and in the way they use their money.

Men recognize that they may lose, but they still play to win. Investing as a zero sum game (meaning "if I win, you lose") may be an extension of competition for power. Accepting possible loss is harder for women, and for some, playing it safe means not investing at all.

Men are usually more aggressive in trying to make their money grow. Women try to keep it safe, to budget so that what they have will suffice. They invariably describe them-

29

selves as "conservative," and their major financial planning objective as "to save." In many cases, this is because women have less money—whether through wages or other sources. Yet I have found the same attitude in women who are very well off and could afford some risk.

It is about 5:00 P.M., and I am getting ready to go home after a long day in the financial market. A woman about forty years of age appears at my office door and says she must speak with me. She says she attended one of my seminars several months ago and knew right then that I was the only person who could help her. She tells me that she is single, a teacher, without much security (a bank account of about $5,000 and a teacher's annuity currently valued at $14,000), but that she recently inherited some money from her father's estate. It is very important to her to do "the right thing." She opens her purse and takes out a number of checks. I add them up mentally as I flip through them—they total $60,000. She tells me that she has been carrying them around in her bag for the past few months because she didn't want to do anything that was too risky, and she didn't know what was the right thing. I ask her what would have happened if someone had stolen her bag. She says she hadn't thought of that.

Few of us, I'm happy to say, would have been as fearful as this woman. Apart from the risk of having it stolen, she was losing money by *not* using it.

Rule Number 1: There is no reward without at least some risk.

Sticking to so-called low-risk investments, checking and savings accounts, certificates of deposit, Treasury bills, and the like will result in a low rate of return. These government insured, interest-focused investments are appropriate for money that you need to keep readily available, when you are looking for an investment opportunity, or when you perceive that safety is appropriate to your financial situation and goals.

After a long discussion with the woman who walked into my office, we decided that her primary goal was to own a home of her own. Her income was sufficient to meet her present living expenses, and part of her inheritance could be used for the down payment on a house, with the balance invested in a government bond that would provide additional interest income.

Her investment stance represented a conservative approach. Given her circumstances and emotional needs, the house was her only "risk" investment. But to her, that was a risk worth taking because she would always have a place of her own in which to live, one that would, hopefully, appreciate in value over the years. She was, indeed, doing the "right thing" by using the money wisely.

RULE NUMBER 2: The greater the reward, usually the higher the risk.

The so-called high-risk investments are the slot machines of the financial world: You can win the jackpot or you can lose your shirt. Investments that carry the highest risk are called "speculations" or "long shots." And, emphatically, women differ from men in the degree of speculation in their investments. Granted, Las Vegas and Atlantic City cater to both genders, but Wall Street speculators, as illustrated by brokerage firm client profiles, are predominantly men. Commodity trading is considered high risk, a zero sum game in which there is one loser for every winner. Playing the game itself is what matters. Competition or excitement is usually the chief motive, although it is a well-known curiosity among brokers that some clients, probably in the minority, speculate in order to lose money. It is said that they "need the pain." *Speculating is for those who can afford to lose it all.*

*   *   *

A divorced mother of three discussed with me her $75,000 money market account. She had no job and her career skills were uncertain. This money was all she had from the sale of her house, which was her divorce settlement. Since her plans were uncertain, and her situation precarious, I recommended very conservative investments. But she was "too afraid" of even this low-risk strategy to take my investment advice.

Later she told me that she talked with another broker, The Magician, who told her that "her problem was that if she never took any risk, she would never get ahead." Her broker advised her to invest *all* her money with him in a partnership that takes advantage of price changes in government paper and foreign currencies. She did not understand this, but was too timid to ask questions. I pointed out to her that this proposal sounded like high-risk commodity trading and was *not appropriate* for her circumstances. But she decided to take the risk.

What she did was equivalent to jumping off a fifty-story building to see if she would land okay. She lived, but not happily ever after. I learned later that she and many others had been victims of a case of commodity trading fraud, and The Magician had made all the money disappear. The woman had made the classic investment errors. The degree of risk in the investment was inappropriate to her financial situation. And she had made only *one* investment, instead of *diversifying* her funds among investments with varying degrees of risk. If she had diversified, at least when the high-risk investment failed she would have had something left.

RULE NUMBER 3: The degree of risk you take should correspond to the amount of money you can afford to lose.

In the game of finance, failure is okay some of the time, especially if you learn a lesson from it. But nobody invests to lose. So along with every investment decision, you should make a very careful and realistic assessment of why you are making that particular decision and what you can reasonably expect to gain or lose.

An exceptional and successful retired businesswoman decided to trade stock options. She had no interest in financial planning since most of her assets were still tied up with her company, but she had a high income and she wanted to trade for high profits—a very aggressive approach.

She talked with me daily, first thing in the morning, to get "quotes," and, as she became more sophisticated, she made decisions using a variety of option strategies. She even phoned me while traveling in Europe, so as not to miss a thing. At first, she made thoughtful and profitable trades. Then she wanted more excitement, became very sure of her infallibility, and took unjustified risks.

It became clear that her trading was just entertainment, and I was "company" for a lonely person. She was no longer trading in a reasonable manner, and her losses began to exceed her "smart money" wins. In the end, this client decided wisely to give up the option trading game for diversions more suited to her wit and savvy.

RULE NUMBER 4: Take and maintain control over your own financial situation.

"Just a minute, I'll put my husband on...." I can't remember how many times I've heard that line over the phone. Why do women have these problems relating to finance? Sometimes it is an old attitude, an inner voice that says, "Take care of me." This may be a difficult feeling to change. All of us have shifts between dependency and independence. They can cause confusion and get us in trouble.

Unfortunately, women alone often regard their own financial management as a temporary stage in life, so they don't pay attention or try to learn what they need to know. The young career woman, the no-longer married, the widow—each may be waiting for someone to come along and take care of it for them. Hopefully, a male someone. Sometimes this person is a broker, a lawyer, an accountant, or a financial planner.

Sometimes it is even another woman.

If the adviser is authoritative, women clients are more likely than men to follow the advice. But by delegating their decision-making to others, women tend to be more easily manipulated. They do not like to anger their advisers—they need them too much. Women clients like to think of their advisers as friends who have their *clients'* best interests at heart.

A brokerage firm is not a public library that provides free information. It is not a doctor's office dispensing prescriptions. A financial planner is not a lawyer, accountant, and clairvoyant market expert all wrapped up in one. Although many financial professionals are knowledgeable, they are still only advisers, not guardians. It is *your* money, *your* choice, *your* future.

You might not be one of these women, but the problem they exemplify is big and real. Women do delegate too much control of their money to others. "Just a minute, I'll put my husband on the phone." Someday he may not be there. Or, "Whatever you say is all right." It may not be.

Mr. and Mrs. Recently Retired come to see me. He explains authoritatively (and inaccurately) his investment portfolio and strategy. He wants continued security for their way of life and specifically wants: liquidity, tax-free income, and low risk. They already own some tax-free bond funds, but he is convinced that they are taxable—and erroneously reports the income to the IRS. The couple owns a large amount of stock in one company for which he worked at one time. Even though this stock does not pay much of a dividend, he has an emotional connection to the company and will not consider diversification.

She sits by, supportively, while I give explanations and make suggestions to improve their understanding and financial situation. I also recommend that Mrs. Retired take a more active role in the decision-making process and learn about what is going on. She protests that she doesn't understand all this, she does not want to know, and that her husband is much better in "these matters." "These matters" is her euphemism for the indelicate subject of money. No action is taken. I telephone about three weeks later. Mr. Retired has died suddenly. What is she to do?

In contrast to the fearful Mrs. Recently Retired, I heard about a woman who used the proceeds of her deceased husband's life insurance to buy a minor league baseball team. That is something most of us would not imagine doing with life insurance proceeds. Yea for her team!

In operating the team with apparent chances of success, she needed to borrow money from the bank. (In the course of her business with the bank, she was allegedly asked if her husband knew what she was doing.) The arrangements with the bank turned out to be a problem. Perhaps the bank was uncertain whether a woman could operate a traditionally male business. I don't know how it all turned out, but her determination to maintain her own financial independence is what is important here.

RULE NUMBER 5: Know your own financial situation, set realistic goals, and assess the amount of risk you are willing or able to take to achieve those goals *before* you begin to play the money game—and review them periodically as your circumstances change.

A young professional woman who had heard me speak at an investment seminar came to see me for financial help. Even though she regularly sent money to relatives in China, she had been able to save enough for the purchase of a condo as well as to establish a significant savings account. Thinking of other clients with the same earning capacity, I didn't know how she had managed to be so frugal. Although she wasn't aware of all the different types of investments that were available, she had a sense of what she wanted. Her goal was to steadily increase her assets, but with risk management in mind. Because she had established this goal, it was easy to help her select appropriate growth stocks and to create a reasonable investment portfolio appropriate to her circumstances. This included a U.S. Treasury note for her "safe money" as an offset to the risk of the stock market. Her strategy was highly successful. She is continuing to add to her investment assets on a planned periodic basis. Since she saves money diligently, weighs the risks before investing, monitors her investments cautiously, and now educates herself about investing, I have no doubt that she will meet her long-term goal of financial security.

RULE NUMBER 6: Seek the best financial advice available, but make your own decisions.

Receiving professional help in managing your finances is not a sign of weakness or dependence. It's just plain common sense unless you have the time and knowledge to become an expert yourself. Still, you must learn how to evaluate guidance and advice, whether from someone across a desk from you, on the other end of the telephone, or talking to you from the TV screen. Is it right for you? What are the alternatives? What are the advantages and disadvantages? If you don't know, ask. If your adviser doesn't know, look for another adviser.

Learning the terminology, reading articles and books, and especially learning not to be afraid of numbers—not even of the "bottom line"—are all important. *Numbers inform.* They are a tool to translate the information into decision-making form.

No one can do these things for you. Experience in dealing with money, like anything else, makes the next time easier.

RULE NUMBER 7: The money game is a business.

For many women, the lack of experience in dealing with businesspeople as equals often leads to demands for extraordinary help. This is probably because of a lifetime of expectations of special treatment at home or in the service industries—beauty salons, clothing stores—that cater to women. Being informed, communicating, and listening to answers is businesslike. Being curt, distrustful, or a "pushover" is not businesslike. There are some fine lines here. You should speak with relaxed authority and know what you are doing, yet be willing to listen to professional help.

It is 5:30 A.M. (Pacific Time). My husband and I are awakened by the telephone. A client is on the line. She is sorry to call me at home, but she's been up all night unable to sleep because someone has solicited her to buy index options. She's been thinking it over and is convinced it's a good idea. The operator at my office had given the client my home phone number after being told that it was urgent that the client reach me in order to make a trade.

Half asleep, I attempt to explain that buying index options is essentially betting whether the stock market will go up or down by a certain date—a very risky proposition. This client is married and both she and her husband are close to retirement; she has always invested conservatively with her modest but comfortable assets and income.

She does not understand my explanation. So I tell her

that I will call her at 7:00 A.M. from my office to go over it with her in detail.

She replies, in an irritated voice, "Don't call me at seven. I haven't slept all night. I'm going back to bed."

You can make better decisions when you ask the right questions. If you consider only the important factors and exclude nonessentials, you can evaluate your options more easily. For example, "But how much do I get each month?" is the wrong question to ask if you are determining the suitability of an investment to provide income. Instead, ask questions about the yield (percentage of return on the dollar amount invested), the length of time before the investment matures, and the quality of the investment. How much you get each month can be figured afterward.

As an illustration, a bond fund bought for $10,350 may pay you $66 a month in interest, or a 7.6 percent annual yield or return on the money you invested ($66 times 12 months equals $792, divided by 10,350 equals 7.6). But if, on maturity, the value of the bonds in the fund is $10,000, your real rate of return will be lower because you will lose $350 of your original investment ($10,350 less $10,000). Asking questions that concern the bottom line is a good way to learn. Note that funds are often quoted with the most favorable yield; these quotes may be misleading.

Financial professionals expect their clients to act in a certain businesslike manner. The rules are not written down anywhere, but they are clearly understood. Much is just a matter of common sense and mutual courtesy. Frequently asking for financial information and service without expecting to pay for them is against the "rules." There is no 411, except at the telephone company, and even they may charge you now. Since financial firms (and banks, too) are sales organizations in business to make a profit, you must expect to pay for their time.

You are also expected to perform under a contract, even an oral one. "I didn't understand," "I've changed my mind," or "I forgot to send the money in time" are all unacceptable behavior. If you don't understand something, say so. Otherwise, the professional has a right to assume you do understand and are making a competent decision. And prompt decisions, once the facts are known, are desirable.

You should also develop a "business sense"—the ability to think bottom line—in handling your financial affairs. That attitude may be more familiar to men, who are often in careers where aggressive behavior is prized, careers that yield experiences in decision-making and gear them toward judgment by positive results.

The point here is not that one type of career or behavior is "better" than another, but that women and men have entirely different systems of confronting life decisions. Women tend to favor conciliation and arbitration, while men seem to favor adversary competition. Men, as a result, play "I win, you lose" games (or business transactions), while women seek accommodation, with both sides giving up something so both may gain. The techniques of good business management are important when dealing with money in the investment world.

To summarize the meaning of the Rules of the Money Game:

- Reward and risk are usually related. A potentially higher reward invites greater risk.
- Do not risk what you can't afford to lose.
- Know your own financial situation. Set realistic goals and plan accordingly.
- Diversification is a risk control strategy.
- Invest appropriately for your circumstances.

- Seek professional advice but maintain control over your own financial decisions.
- Ask questions that concern the bottom line.
- Numbers help to make decisions.
- Businesslike behavior is required in dealing with financial professionals and in managing your own money.

Beyond these general rules, women must always remember that the game of finance is played to win. This does not mean that we must gamble, or cannot be on the team. It simply means we must understand the gamesmanship that goes along with money management, always keeping our own personal objectives in mind when dealing with the financial world.

One good way to begin is by learning what money really means to you. What are your goals in life, and what financial goals must you set to achieve them? The answers to those questions are the first step in making your own financial plan.

4

Follow the Yellow Brick Road

PLANNING REALISTIC FINANCIAL GOALS

A couple comes to see me. The husband is starting his practice as a plastic surgeon, his wife is a consultant. They are very pleasant, warm, and open people. This is a second marriage for both, and they are starting over in a new location in a rented house. In organizing a financial plan for this well-meaning couple, I notice that all their assets are in cash, about $150,000.

Their stated and sincere financial goal is to be worth a million dollars in about one and a half years, and double that in five. I am dumbfounded. Even with sensational earnings in their careers, plus their present asset base, it doesn't seem possible. Of course, there is an outside chance of luck at the gambling table or winning a lottery, but they are not the type for these activities. Their goal is hardly realistic. I make some suggestions that I feel are more sensible, but they go away disillusioned with me.

I can't spin straw into gold. However, Rumpelstiltskin, whom they meet next, says he can. About a year later, they are back in my office with no assets. Rumpelstiltskin, it seems, advised them to buy precious stones. They did, and they were not. They are both now making money, and their earnings will give them a second chance, but their goals are realistic and their funds invested wisely.

We all have goals in our lives. Generally, we concentrate on the small, day-to-day goals—scheduling our social events and appointments, saving for a vacation—and neglect focusing on the big, important ones—improving or maintaining a life-style of choice. In fact, these goals may seem vague and unclear to us.

In order to establish and clarify our goals, we need to think about them consciously and realistically. (I am prejudiced in favor of realism!) There is a difference between dreams and goals. Being rich, famous, and thin may not be in the cards for all of us, but being financially secure, happy, and healthier is certainly possible.

DREAMS + REALISM = GOALS
PRAGMATISM (SENSIBLE, PRACTICAL PLANNING) GETS YOU THERE

Achieving your financial goals can be the key to achieving other life goals even though the two are not the same. Money affects the quality of our lives. We may not choose to concentrate on finances most of the time, but we need to recognize three things: First, money is an appropriate subject for women. Second, we don't have to make financial decisions based on someone else's idea—internal parent, accountant—of how we "should" regard money. And third, good financial housekeeping can help achieve our other life goals.

Samantha Solvent, age twenty-seven, is an accountant with a practical attitude toward money and finance. Since beginning a high-paying job after college, she has saved a good chunk of each month's salary. She now has $10,000. Her objective: to buy a condo for investment and security, and so she won't have to pay rent.

But several family tragedies have caused Samantha to change her priorities. "I want to travel," she now says, "and also spend more time with my father. I'll always earn a good salary. I can buy a condo when I'm older." New objective: Samantha is taking her recently widowed father on a trip to Africa.

Because of her original savings success, Samantha is able to rearrange her goals. She acknowledges that her new plan is less rewarding in dollars, but says, "There are other kinds of return on an investment in traveling the world and being with family." As a young career woman with good earnings and an immediate need for cash for traveling, she should consider a low-risk investment that pays a moderate rate of interest and can be liquidated instantly.

What are your expectations? Retirement in a lounge chair at the beach? Travel on a camel near the Nile? The independence of home ownership? To do any or all of these things you need money. To have the right amount of money when you need it means you must make financial plans, and *act on them.*

Start at the beginning by clarifying the life goals that motivate you. It may be difficult, but it is very important to know what you want out of life before you think of money.

Take the time to give your life goals some serious thought. Even if you are on the fast track in the career you always wanted, or married to a successful man, look at your present and future life through a wide-angle lens. It is the essential first step to good financial planning. Write your goals down, preferably in a looseleaf notebook that will permit you to add pertinent articles and outside information as you develop your financial plan and achieve your life goals. The writing process itself helps to clarify goals since you must reduce complicated thoughts to a few words. I recommend a six-step process.

STEP 1: MY LIFE GOALS

Another way of knowing what you want out of life is saying "what you want to be." How you get what you want to be is by taking action. So title your first page, My Life Goals. Now make two columns, labeled "I Want to Be" and "By Doing."

As an example, I've illustrated my goals just as they came to me. You will want to draw up your own.

My Life Goals

I Want to Be	*By*
Free	Working independently
Healthy	Eating right
Secure	Succeeding financially
Loving	Caring about others
Knowledgeable	Reading and learning
Attractive	Exercising
Experienced	Traveling and observing

This is an important start to the planning process. Sometimes your first thoughts are the most accurate, so don't edit them yet. When you have completed your list, review it and decide if your life goals are realistic. Be very frank and honest with yourself. Your secret childhood dream may have been to be a famous artist. You must decide whether to include that as a life goal or simply retain it as a lovely fantasy.

Cross out those goals that are not realistic, and that are someone else's expectations for you.

I think this is another special female concern, a holdover from our childhood training to please others.

STEP 2: MY FINANCIAL GOALS

Now start a new list, this time heading it "My Financial Goals." These goals are related to those life goals that have to do with money or are dependent on money. For example, Yvonne Target, a thirty-seven-year-old lawyer, divorced with a child, listed "security" as her primary life goal. These were her financial goals:

Buy a house

Educate her child

Pay off debts

Increase her asset base for investment potential

Keep up with inflation (she is very sensitive to this)

Emergency fund

Retirement security (but she is more interested in her child's education—and her own possible remarriage)

STEP 3: MY SHORT-TERM AND LONG-TERM FINANCIAL GOALS

Armed with the information and self-knowledge gained in the first two steps, you should now decide *when* you want to achieve your financial goals. You may want to achieve some of them soon. However you define "soon," these will be your short-term goals. Those to be achieved farther in the future are your long-term goals. Some may have both short- and long-term aspects.

Of the financial goals Yvonne Target listed, buying a home is short-term, her child's education is long-term, and her desire to keep up with inflation is both.

Now take your own list of financial goals and do the same thing.

STEP 4: PRIORITIZE YOUR GOALS

The next step is to decide which of these goals is the most important, and then rank the rest in descending order. For example, after the house and education goals, Yvonne wants to reduce her debts. Retirement is her least important goal *at this time.*

You'll be surprised at how prioritizing your goals brings everything into focus. You now know more about yourself and your goals than most women do, and have a clear and realistic idea of what you want.

STEP 5: KNOW YOUR FINANCIAL RISK ORIENTATION

In our example, now that Yvonne Target has prioritized her goals, she can make a financial plan to achieve them. She has a relatively high-risk approach to her planning because of her young age, strong earning capacity, and the pension established by her law firm. Also, because she establishes security first, she makes an unusually large down payment on a house—50 percent of the cash settlement from her divorce. She allocates the rest this way: 15 percent for her child's college fund (her ex-spouse contributes the same); 5 percent for emergencies; 25 percent for high-risk growth stocks; and 5 percent to reduce her debts. Her savings each month will add to her growth stock portfolio, or other investments as they seem appropriate and as her salary increases.

Like Yvonne, examine your goals along with your existing assets. Then establish the degree of risk you are willing to take. Ask yourself what part of your assets you don't want to take a chance with. (You may reconsider this question after you complete the next chapter, which shows you how to evaluate your assets.)

Martha Mature, a widow, age sixty, comes to me with a goal but no way of achieving it. Martha has inherited $185,000 in liquid assets—stocks and certificates of deposit. Her goal: Though she has a rent-controlled apartment, she wants to buy a co-op in New York. She does not own a car. She still needs enough money for living expenses, and wants to spend winters in Hollywood, Florida. The present cost of housing in New York makes this goal unaffordable. In fact, her income from investments and Social Security do not presently allow Martha the luxury of wintering in Florida. As a result, she is "dipping into capital"—that is, she is spending a portion of her assets, thus reducing the income derived from those assets. What follows is an abbreviated version of what her cash flow, or the plus and minus difference between her income and her expenses, looks like:

Annual income:	
Social Security	$ 6,900
Stocks and 6-month CDs	10,800
Total	$17,700
Annual expenses:	
Rent ($475/month)	$ 5,700
All other living costs	9,000
Travel to Florida	5,000
Total	$19,700

Martha was surprised and disappointed that she was living beyond her income and could not afford to buy the co-op. But just in passing she mentioned another goal: to continue renting in New York and buy a condo in Florida. That goal might be realistic because she can rent the condo for the nine months out of the year that she isn't there.

Cost of Florida condo, cash (no mortgage)	$85,000
9-month rental income from condo (less monthly common charges)	$ 4,500
Income from the remaining $100,000 in capital in low-risk investments (approximately 9% at that time)	$ 9,000
Total rental/investment income	$13,500
Plus Social Security	6,900
Total income	$20,400

Martha can use her rental and investment income for living expenses, while her Social Security can be earmarked for her rented apartment with some extra to spare. She can spend the winters "free" in her Florida condo, or afford to continue her present Florida arrangement. Her condo will also serve as a backup residence if she ever decides to leave New York.

Martha can meet her life and financial goals with this low-risk investment plan. She will be able to sleep better at night with insured bank accounts or government notes, rather than betting on the stock market, and lead the life she wants. Without such a plan, she would have to make some hard choices before she cannibalized her assets. In my opinion, a major commitment in the stock market is not appropriate for Martha, who is no longer working and in need of a dependable income. Though the market may provide her with some increased asset values, it represents continued risk.

Mr. and Mrs. Allornothing are aged fifty and fifty-two, respectively. Their goal, as they told it to me, is to "get out of the stock market in one year and switch to ultra-conservative, income-producing investments." Sounds reasonable. They are totally liquid at the moment. They are negative toward all real estate and are canceling their life insurance policies. My eyebrows go up!

Assets:
    Cash in bank $ 100,000
    Six stocks   1,000,000
Liabilities: 0
Annual Income: 35,000

Highly unusual, I think. The six stocks are all extremely speculative, high-risk investments. Only three are showing a profit at this time. A few months later, things are not going too well. During a phone call, I hear Mr. Allornothing yelling in the background while his wife asks me for quotes on their stocks.

I don't know if the Allornothings got out of the market in one year and are now ultraconservative investors. Somehow, I doubt it. They were gambling, not investing. They were not open to any suggestions of goal changes. If you do not try to achieve your goals within a realistic framework, they will probably go awry.

STEP 6: REVIEW YOUR GOALS PERIODICALLY

Take a fresh look at your goals periodically, perhaps once a year, and update your notebook if necessary. Note your accomplishments as well as any changes in priority. You are now a woman in control because you are doing something toward understanding and achieving your important goals. You know which are realistic, which the most important, and which the most immediate. And with a longer-term focus, you know where you want to go.

Now that you know your ultimate objective, the next stage of financial planning is examining where you are right now. You need to check the pantry before you go to shop for a dinner party.

CHAPTER

Where Am I?

YOUR ASSETS AND LIABILITIES

WE all think we know what we are worth. However, we're usually wrong. Most women don't bother to figure it out on paper, but it is a good idea, and a necessity if you are going to make a realistic financial plan to achieve your life goals. If you don't know where you are, you can't know where you're going.

Ms. Worried Lady comes to see me to achieve what she calls "financial balance." She feels her finances are too complicated. She is about fifty years old, her children are out of the house, and she is separated and living in Florida. Her husband, a banker living in Connecticut, will not give her enough money to live on, and she has not found a job. Ms. Worried Lady does not have an attorney; she is uncertain about divorce and considers her husband to be "honorable." She would like to sell their house. He refuses.

Ms. Worried Lady isn't quite sure what they own or what their financial status is. At my request, she is able to get partial information from her husband, though he is reluctant to provide it:

ASSETS

Joint liquid assets	about	$ 60,000
Her own liquid assets		500
Residence, jointly owned, market value		225,000
Husband's IRA		6,000
Husband's life insurance cash value		unknown
Husband's liquid assets		unknown

LIABILITIES (all joint)

Mortgage	$ 7,000
Credit cards	8,000
Home improvement loan	3,000
School loans for children	30,000
Autos	25,000

JOINT NET WORTH (assets – liabilities)
Joint assets exclude her liquid assets and husband's
IRA funds.

$ 212,000

I note the use of debt financing for consumer goods. Ms.
Worried Lady's estranged husband has told her that it is
smart to borrow because of the tax deductions; this,
however, was prior to the tax law changes having to do with
interest and finance charges. In fact, such borrowing actually
reduces their visible net worth.

Husband's income (annual salary)	$ 77,000
Her income (annual allowance)	10,000

Out of balance, out of control. It turns out that by
"financial balance," Ms. Worried Lady means that she
doesn't understand her finances and she is not in control of
her security. She signs tax returns without reading them.
She has always delegated her financial security to her
husband.

There is nothing else I can do for Ms. Worried Lady. I
cannot give her financial advice until it is clear what assets
she controls. At this point, she controls only her cash

"allowance." It is my guess that her husband is intentionally keeping her in the dark about their finances. I recommend that she find a good attorney.

To find out where you are, you have to ask yourself the right questions. If necessary, at this point in establishing your own financial knowledge, ask your husband, father, lawyer, broker, financial adviser, or anyone else concerned with your financial situation.

In actuality, of course, your financial situation is constantly changing. The concept here is to stop the clock, to temporarily freeze your numbers so you can take inventory. At this moment in time ask yourself, What do I have? What am I worth? The answers provide what is called a *net worth statement*. You don't need to detail your net worth down to the last nickel. But a "fix" on some rounded numbers is essential for the purpose of realistic financial planning. What you have or own are your *assets*. What you owe are your *liabilities*. The difference between the two is your *net worth*.

$$\text{Assets} - \text{Liabilities} = \text{Net Worth}$$

Your net worth is hopefully a positive number. But if you have more liabilities than assets, you can have a negative net worth. Many women in the beginning of their careers are in this situation because of school and auto loans. In such cases, one of your financial goals may be budget management. Whether your net worth is positive or negative, it is where you are—financially.

It's time to make another list. (List making is my commonsense approach to everything—a woman's sense of order.) Let's look at how to list your net worth.

We begin with your assets. Divide your assets into three categories:

1. Assets that are liquid, or *short-term,* are quickly salable and easily converted to cash. You can get your hands on it for that winter trip or emergency car repair. For example, a savings account, money market fund, stock or bond is usually thought of as liquid or short-term. You can go to the bank and get it out, or pick up the phone and sell it instantly.

2. Assets that are *longer-term,* or less liquid. Real estate and business ownership are longer-term assets, less quickly salable.

3. *Noninvestment assets* are items of value that you own but are unlikely to sell in order to invest the proceeds— your furniture or your car for instance.

For the purpose of determining your net worth, list both your short-term and longer-term assets, but exclude your noninvestment assets from your financial planning. You should, however, include them whenever you apply for a loan at the bank.

The value you assign to each of your short-term and longer-term assets must be what they would be worth if you were to cash them in or sell them today—*not* what you paid for them or what they will be worth in the future. This is called *market value.* If your assets are in bank accounts, stocks, bonds, and the like, you can estimate their market value by using bank, brokerage, and insurance statements.

Fig. 5–1 on page 58 describes the information shown on a typical broker's confirmation of a sale or purchase of securities; Fig. 5–2 on page 59 shows the content of a typical brokerage statement and how to read it. To determine the current value of securities you may own, you can use quotes printed in the newspaper—Figs. 5–3 and 5–4, pages 61 and 62, show how to read these. I have included these samples because financial statements and newspaper reports with their imaginative abbreviations and unfamiliar computer formats are not always easy to interpret and can be confusing to new investors. The size of the print doesn't help either!

A TYPICAL NET WORTH STATEMENT

A young career woman in public relations, lets call her P.R.,
lists her assets like this, as of today:

ASSETS:
  1. Short-term

Checking account	$ 380
Money market fund	2,000
Savings account	1,800
Mutual fund	3,250
Loan to brother	750
Total short-term assets	$ 8,180

P.R. has quickly found the first three figures from the
monthly bank statement she receives. For the value of her
mutual fund, she turns to the financial pages of her
newspaper and finds its per-unit value as of the close of
yesterday's market. She takes the number of units she owns
from the statement she receives and multiplies it by the net
asset value (NAV) listed in the paper. The NAV is the price
at which each unit can be sold: 100 units at a NAV of $32.50
is $3,250.

  2. Long-term

Pension	2,000
Total long-term asset	2,000

  3. Noninvestment assets

Auto	4,000

(P.R. found the value of her auto in the *Kelly Blue Book*
at the library.) She estimates the value of her household
furnishings at their possible worth as used items.

Household furnishings 3,000

Finally, she lists the jewelry, which she recently inherited, at the value assigned by the estate documents.

Jewelry	2,500
Total noninvestment assets	9,500
Total assets	$19,680
Total assets for financial planning (total assets	
– noninvestment assets)	$10,180

LIABILITIES

Auto loan @10% due 23 mo.	2,800
Credit cards @19%	800
School loan @9%	1,200
Total liabilities	$ 4,800
Total net worth (total assets – total liabilities)	$14,880
Net worth for financial planning (total net	
worth – total noninvestment assets)	$ 5,380

Note that P.R.'s total assets for financial planning are only about a third of her net worth. She may prefer to think herself as rich as the larger number, but in reality she must work with the smaller one. Note, too, that your liabilities can be broken down into short- and long-term if it clarifies things for you, but more important, write down the interest rate you are paying and due date, if any, on outstanding loans—a consideration for payoff priorities.

THE NET WORTH FORMAT

Fig. 5–5 at the end of this chapter is a format for the listing of assets and liabilities, employing the specific categories commonly used by financial professionals. Use it as a guide when you prepare your own net worth statement. It may remind you of some assets and liabilities you forgot, such as pension plans or old debts to Aunt Tillie, or some that I haven't thought of. It's important to list everything.

You also need good descriptions of what you own and what you owe. For an asset this includes: the date acquired, the exact and complete name, and the amount. For example:

Bond (face value, full title, interest rate or coupon, due date)
   Example: $25,000 State of X.X. various purpose, dated 1/1/84, registered 8.375%, due 1/1/04
Unit trust (name and number)
   Example: 10 units Municipal Trust Fund #29 monthly payment series
Preferred stock (name and number)
   Example: 200 shares of MNO 7.50% convertible preferred 1st series group 5
Common stock (name and number of shares including reinvested ones, stock dividends, splits)
   Example: 280 shares of QRZ
Bank certificate of deposit (amount, name of bank, rate of interest, due date)
   Example: $10,000, 3rd National Bank, @ 7.75%, due 1/15/88

A good description of a liability includes:

Amount originally owed and to whom
      Last Mortgage Company $75,000
Interest rate: 12%
Date of maturity: 6/1/03
Timing and amounts of repayment—principal and interest: monthly amount $000

RECORD KEEPING

Unfortunately, I've noticed that women are particularly negligent in keeping good financial records. Many a client has brought me her records in boxes, envelopes, bags—and admits to not reading or understanding them. Perhaps this is due to lack of experience with business records. Before I went into brokering, my own method was outrageous. I stuffed papers into drawers (different drawers for different papers) until tax time, and then took the contents of the right drawers to an accountant. The notebook method, even for receipts, is now my favorite.

Your net worth statement is one of the most useful records you can keep. A notebook is also helpful for this purpose. Although right now you are interested in finding out where you are financially, your circumstances may change. And with changing circumstances come changing financial priorities. So keep your net worth statement current.

Finally, it is important, when listing your financial assets, to note who owns them. Are they yours alone? Are they joint ownership with rights of survivorship, tenants in common, the family trust? If they are held with someone else, note how much is yours (50 percent?). You should know who can take action on the asset. For instance, a savings account may require the signature of each owner for withdrawals, but most brokerage joint accounts require only one voice. The same holds true for liabilities. Know the circumstances under which you may be held liable for your husband's debts, or the debts incurred by a business with a partner.

When it comes to managing money, organization is good financial housekeeping. Like a modicum of orderliness at home, it makes life much simpler. You will start *thinking* in an organized manner that is very helpful in making financial decisions. It will also help you at tax time.

You should now have a list of your financial goals as well as an inventory of your assets and liabilities. You know your net worth. And when you measure that against your goals, you should have some idea of how realistic they are in light of the amount of risk you are willing to take. Now your financial picture doesn't seem so overwhelming and out of control. But before you proceed with your financial plan, you still need several more pieces of information:

Fig. 5–1 Contents of a Broker's Confirmation

① Purchase date: 11-11-86
② Security name and title: Anonymous Limited ③b
③a Price per share: 33 1/4 ($33.25) and total: $3,325
  Yield to maturity (if it is a bond or debt instrument): This is a stock so there is no yield to maturity; dividend yields are not indicated on common stock confirmations.
④ Commission (unless a net trade, in which case the commission is already calculated as part of the price): $44.
⑤ Total trade price (the cost you need for tax purposes): $3,369

Bonds and over-the-counter stocks are usually traded at net price. Stocks traded on the stock exchange show a commission separate from the price.

This is all the information you need to enter the purchase into your records for later determination of profit or loss and exactly what it is you bought or sold.

Your monthly statement will reflect the trade as part of its "activity" for the month, but it may not be a complete description. It is a very important record to keep. Again, a looseleaf notebook works best because it allows you to find information easily.

Fig. 5–2 Contents of a Broker's Monthly Statement

(For clarity, I am using an illustration with minimal activity. This statement happens to be an IRA account.)

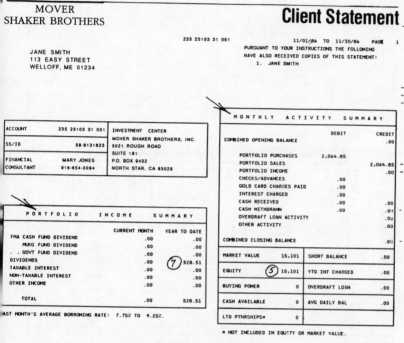

MOVER
SHAKER BROTHERS

Client Statement

235 25103 31 051

11/01/86 TO 11/30/86   PAGE   1
PURSUANT TO YOUR INSTRUCTIONS THE FOLLOWING
HAVE ALSO RECEIVED COPIES OF THIS STATEMENT:
1. JANE SMITH

JANE SMITH
113 EASY STREET
WELLOFF, ME 01234

ACCOUNT	235 25103 31 051	INVESTMENT CENTER
SS/ID	59-9131823	MOVER SHAKER BROTHERS, INC.
		5021 ROUGH ROAD
		SUITE 181
FINANCIAL	MARY JONES	P.O. BOX 9432
CONSULTANT	916-654-0094	NORTH STAR, CA 83029

MONTHLY ACTIVITY SUMMARY

	DEBIT	CREDIT
COMBINED OPENING BALANCE		.00
PORTFOLIO PURCHASES	2,064.85	
PORTFOLIO SALES		2,064.85
PORTFOLIO INCOME		.00
CHECKS/ADVANCES	.00	
GOLD CARD CHARGES PAID	.00	
INTEREST CHARGED	.00	
CASH RECEIVED	.00	.00
CASH WITHDRAWN	.00	.00
OVERDRAFT LOAN ACTIVITY		.00
OTHER ACTIVITY		.00
COMBINED CLOSING BALANCE		.00

MARKET VALUE	15,101	SHORT BALANCE	.00
EQUITY	15,101	YTD INT CHARGED	.00
BUYING POWER	0	OVERDRAFT LOAN	.00
CASH AVAILABLE	0	AVG DAILY BAL	.00
LTD PTNRSHIPS*	0		

* NOT INCLUDED IN EQUITY OR MARKET VALUE.

PORTFOLIO INCOME SUMMARY

	CURRENT MONTH	YEAR TO DATE
FMA CASH FUND DIVIDEND	.00	.00
MUNI FUND DIVIDEND	.00	.00
. . GOVT FUND DIVIDEND	.00	.00
DIVIDENDS	.00	528.51
TAXABLE INTEREST	.00	.00
NON-TAXABLE INTEREST	.00	.00
OTHER INCOME	.00	.00
TOTAL	.00	528.51

LAST MONTH'S AVERAGE BORROWING RATE: 7.75% TO 9.25%.

FOR ACCOUNT OF:

BANK OF HOPE TTEE
FBO JANE SMITH
IRA DTD 9/16/82
P.O. BOX 92918
HOPE, CA 83129

The monthly statement a brokerage firm sends to clients includes the following information:

➤ *Monthly Activity* is summarized on page 1 and is detailed on page 2 as ➤ *"transaction analysis"*: what is going on during this time period.

Trades may include:

① Date of trade: 11/26/86
  Yield, if purchase of a bond or debt instrument (this one is a stock sale)

MOVER
SHAKER BROTHERS   **Client Statement**

BANK OF HOPE TTEE   235 25103 31 051   11/01/86 TO 11/30/86   PAGE 2

↘ **T R A N S A C T I O N   A N A L Y S I S**

TYP	DATE	QUANTITY BOT/RECD	QUANTITY SOLD/DEL	DESCRIPTION	ENTRY/ PRICE	AMOUNT	BALANCES CASH	FUND
				···· OPENING BALANCES ····			.00	
1	11/14/86 ①			SHAKER DAILY DIVIDEND INC DIV REINVESTED $1.97	DIVIDEND	④ 1.97CR	.00	
1	11/26/86		② 25	WELLKNOWN INC ODD LOT · EXECUTED AS AGY SAXP IS A MARKET MAKER	84 1/2	③ 2,064.85CR		2,064.85CR
1	11/28/86			SHAKER DAILY DIVIDEND INC	INVESTMENT	⑥ 2,064.85	.00	
				···· CLOSING BALANCES ····			.00	

↘ **P O R T F O L I O   A N A L Y S I S**

TYP	QUANTITY	DESCRIPTION	PRICE	VALUE	PORT CD	%	ANNUAL DIV/INT	⑧ IND. INCOME	INCOME % YLD	S&P RTG	IND EARNINGS PER SHR	P/E
1	50	ANY CORP	67.87	3,393	58	22.5	3.30	165.00	4.8	A+	4.13	16
1	50	SOME CORP	69.25	3,462	58	22.9	3.60	180.00	5.1	A	7.79	9
1	200	UNDERHAND RESOURCES CORP	4.62	925	99	6.1	.00	.00	.0	NR	4.11-	
1	50	··· WOODEN SHOE WATER CO· N Y REGISTRY-10 GUILDERS	92.87	4,643	58	30.7	5.28	264.40	5.6	A	8.54	11
1	2,676	··· FUND POSITIONS ··· SHAKER DAILY DIVIDEND INC INCLUDES ACCRUED DIVIDENDS FROM 10/11/86 THRU 11/14/86 AVG YIELD FOR PERIOD 5.24%	1.00	2,676	SA	17.7	.00	.00	.0		.00	
		TOTALS		⑤ 15,101		100.0		609.40				

US WITH UP-TO-THE-MINUTE INFORMATION. PRICES ARE PROVIDED ONLY AS A GENERAL GUIDE TO PORTFOLIO VALUE.
BOND PRICES MAY DIFFER FROM CURRENT MARKET QUOTES. COMPUTERIZED PRICING SERVICES ARE OFTEN UNABLE TO SUPPLY
US WITH UP-TO-THE-MINUTE INFORMATION. PRICES ARE PROVIDED ONLY AS A GENERAL GUIDE TO PORTFOLIO VALUE.

I N D U S T R Y   C L A S S I F I C A T I O N

CODE	INDUSTRY	PORT %	VALUE	CODE	INDUSTRY	PORT %	VALUE
58	OIL & GAS	1.76	11,500	SA	MONEY FUNDS	7.71	2,676
99	UNCLASSIFIED ISSUES	6.1	925				

② Description of security: 25 shares, Wellknown, Inc.
Price per unit paid: not on sale statement, but record of
purchase will be on purchase statement
③ Net price paid or received after commissions: $2,064.85

Your cost for tax purposes when purchasing a security is the
price plus commission. Your value for tax purposes when selling
a security is the price received after the commission is deducted.
An IRA account would have different rules, but you will still need
these records.

Other monthly activities include:

Stock splits: none in this case
④ Dividends and interest paid: only $1.97 from money
   market
Checks sent and received: none this month

Portfolio Value: what it's worth (generally on the front page as "equity" as well as "totals" of security positions in the "portfolio analysis"), at current market value the day it was compiled: ⑤$15,101

Other important financial happenings in the ➤"portfolio analysis": ⑥ cash credits ($2,064.85 invested in a money market fund from the sale of the stock) and debits; interest charges, if any; and ⑦ details on dividends and interest computed to an annual value, noted on page 1 under ➤"Portfolio Income Summary." Indicated income ⑧ means annual income at currently announced dividend and interest rates.

Every brokerage firm has its own statement design and its own terminology and various "extras," but these basics should be included.

Fig. 5–3 Stock Exchange

Name	Div.	Yld.	P/E Ratio	Sales 100s	High	Low	Close	Net Chg
Humng	1.80	5.8	13	451	45 5/8	44 3/4	45 1/2	+ 3/8

Name: The name of a security—in this instance it's Humongous, Inc.—is abbreviated; this abbreviation is not the ticker symbol that your broker reads.

Yield: The ratio of the sale price of a single share of stock to the annual dividend it pays per share.

Price/earnings-ratio: The ratio of sale price (P) of all of the outstanding shares of the company to the annual earnings (E) of the company.

Sales 100s: The number of shares traded, in batches or "round lots" of 100 shares. On this day, 45,100 shares of Humongous, Inc., were traded.

High: The highest price during the trading day at which a share of stock was bought or sold.

Low: The lowest price during the trading day.

Close: The price of the final trade of the day.

Net change: The increase or decrease in the stock's price over the prior day's close.

Fig. 5–4   Mutual Funds

Name	NAV	Offer Price	NAV Chg
Octopus Fd	21.66	23.67	–.06

Name: The name of the fund, often abbreviated.

Net asset value (NAV): The collective value of everything in the fund's portfolio, divided by the number of units in the fund. Also called the "bid" or "sell" price.

Offer: net asset value plus sales charge (if any). Also called the "buy" or "asked" price.

NAV change: The increase or decrease in the net asset value since the end of the prior trading day.

Fig. 5–5   Where Am I Now?

ASSETS
  Short-term (liquid) assets
   cash, money market funds
   bank accounts, CDs
   government securities
   bonds
   stocks
   unit trusts
   mutual funds
   trust deeds/mortgages if marketable
   cash value of life insurance or annuities that can be
     cashed in*
   gold/silver bullion or certificates representing bullion
     commodities
   options
  Total liquid assets

  Long-term assets
   real estate
   pensions and profit-sharing plans
   IRA/KEOGH plans
   partnerships
   personal property
   collectibles, jewelry
   trusts, annuities
   business interests
  Total long-term assets

  Total assets

LIABILITIES
    mortgages
    loans, notes
    margin debt
    credit cards
  Total liabilities

NET WORTH (assets less liabilities)

*Note: The face value of life insurance is considered an asset only for
estate tax purposes.

Go with the Flow

YOUR INCOME AND OUTGO

A close relative, recently widowed, came to me for financial advice. I was surprised to learn that in spite of a lifetime of success in an intellectual career, her husband had handled all their finances and she didn't know where to begin. Foremost on her mind was the question "What can I afford?" She had always gauged her spending habits on her husband's values and judgment.

I sat down with her, brought out pencil and paper, and we put her financial goals in writing. She had never thought about them except in very general terms. She accepted one of her husband's conservative tenets: always maintain principal and save a percentage of your income, consistent with the rate of inflation.

When we put numbers on her cash flow, what she had for income and what it cost her to live in the style to which she was accustomed, she had no problem. We also wrote down everything she owned and owed, so she had an understanding of where she stood in an easy format that she helped create. This easy exercise, a simplified financial plan, relieved her mind. Because it was an emotionally stressful time for her, I was very happy to find something to make it easier. Fortunately, she could afford to do most of what she wished. As an added bonus, she gained new confidence, since she could now keep her own records for future information and accounting needs.

Traditionally, numbers have been in the male realm. But to be in control of their own finances, women must also learn to "think in numbers"; it is the way to translate information so that you can make useful comparisons. Numbers help you make rational decisions.

From the previous chapter, you know the numbers for your *net asset value*—what you own and owe. For sound financial planning, these numbers need to be supplemented with numbers about your *cash flow*—what you earn, what you spend, and what you save. Yes, you need to confront the issue of where what one of my former clients referred to as all the "walking-around money" goes.

CASH FLOW AT A GLANCE

Take out your financial notebook and begin to compile the figures for everything you earn and everything you spend. Think a year at a time. This gives you the most complete picture because it takes into account seasonal variations (like heating bills) and payments made irregularly, or quarterly, as well as monthly.

To help you find all sources of income, look at last year's tax return. If this is the first time you have ever really read it, it will be revealing. All your taxable income should be there. To complete your list, add any nontaxable income you receive (child support, municipal bond income, certain pensions, gifts). If your income will remain the same as last year's, fine. If not, estimate this year's income; make sure to include any new sources of income or a cost-of-living increase in your salary or pension. If you wish, you can also make a column for projections for next year.

To jog your memory, here is a list of possible categories of income:

Salaries, commissions, fees

Business income

Pensions

Royalties (books, oil wells)

Rents

Bonuses/awards

Capital gains (sale of real estate, stocks, bonds, collectibles, partnerships, business interests)

Alimony or child support

Gifts (regarded as income for cash flow)

Trusts

Social Security/government benefits

Annuities

Interest/dividends, tax-free interest

You may have others.

Estimating your outgo is a little trickier, since we are all good at forgetting the discretionary expenditures, the same way I forget the extra "nibbles" when I'm dieting. Nevertheless, with the help of your checkbook (which is very revealing), some rough estimates, and the following categories, you should be able to come up with a figure that is close enough.

I like to think of outgo as divided into two categories: *basic expenses* and *discretionary expenses*. This way I can separate in my mind what I absolutely need from what I want. The division also makes me contemplate more carefully before I spend money on extras.

Basic expenses include food, clothes, transportation to work (car, train, bus), rent or maintenance and mortgage, utilities, insurance (life, car, home, health, disability, liability), basic medical and dental outlay beyond insurance coverage, child support, debts, and don't forget taxes (income, property, FICA, or Social Security). Taxes count in this list even if they are deducted from your paycheck.

Discretionary expenses include home maintenance and repair, body maintenance and repair, laundry, donations, dues, vacations, subscriptions, entertainment, gifts, home furnishings, education, retirement contributions, and the ever popular miscellaneous.

Now you have a complete list of your income and your outgo. The rest is easy.

$$\text{Income} - \text{Outgo} = \text{Cash flow}$$
$$\$\$\$ - \$\$ = \$$$

If the difference is a surplus, it's called savings. You have a positive cash flow. If you have a deficit, it's called trouble. You have a negative cash flow. Obviously, if your cash flow is on the plus side, you have more flexibility in planning to achieve your financial goals. If you have a deficit, your financial plan should probably include a budget to help you decrease your spending or find a way to increase your income.

A beautiful, divorced woman in her forties, with no children, came to me for financial advice. She was worried about whether she could "make it" on her expected settlement. She would have an income of about $40,000 a year until her ex-husband's retirement; at that time she would share in the pension plan from his law partnership. She was to keep her luxury car and the house and furnishings—a total worth of about $800,000. The mortgage was approximately $220,000 at a 9 percent fixed rate. She also had a bank account worth $25,000 earmarked for emergencies.

Cash flow was a big problem in her mind since she was used to paying for many personal services, country club, and elaborate vacations. Thinking that her settlement was very substantial, I commented that I thought she would do fine. She still wasn't sure, explaining that just washing her windows, which faced the waterfront, was a major expense. "The sea gulls, you know, are very messy."

So we put a pencil to it—and she was right. Although she could meet her expenses with her present income, the margin was narrow enough to make her feel uncomfortable. Her house expenses and tax liabilities used up most of her income. A rearrangement of her assets and liabilities for better cash flow was necessary. So she decided that selling the house and buying a smaller place made more sense.

After sale of the house, deducting capital gains tax and paying off the mortgage, she had $440,000 plus her $25,000 bank account—total investment capital: $465,000. With that she was able to buy a new luxury condominium. This strategy reduced her residential expenses significantly without really changing her life-style, other than the view of the sea gulls. It also provided her with more liquidity, yielding the desired cash flow so she could live the way she wished, some diversification for safety, and investment capital for growth. Building cash flow is easier, of course, when you have the assets, but without planning, she might have been "cash poor" by her needs and standards.

If your financial goal is to increase your assets, your cash flow should, of course, end up with a surplus. This is money you do not have to spend—money that you can save. And it is from your savings that you can acquire assets—stocks, bonds, real estate, and the like, or even something as simple as a savings account from which you will derive additional income.

To achieve this desirable surplus, use your common

sense. Note which expenditures can be reduced or eliminated. Reconsider what you really "need." Consider what you would like to save. After determining your minimum savings goal, use the discipline of paying your savings account first, before you spend it. This is a way to keep savings safe from spending for anything but an emergency, and you can define emergency ahead of time. Be realistic about uncertain sources of income. For instance, if your ex is a "slow pay" on alimony or child support, include in your income statement the amount you can actually count on, not the amount you're supposed to receive.

On the other hand, if you are lucky enough to have a surplus without much trouble, you can use it to further your financial goals. But if you're like most of us, even with savings and income from other assets, you will have to make some choices—say, foregoing the home improvement in favor of the trip you feel is more important. Or you might choose to cancel some of the entertainment and earmark more savings toward your retirement.

Not everyone wants or needs to live within a disciplined budget. An annual review of your cash flow can tell you what you need to know. Numbers change. The point is that without the numbers in front of you, you can't make intelligent choices. You are not planning at all.

To review:

- You now have your life goals in writing, from which you have highlighted your financial goals.

- You have given some consideration to your concept and tolerance of risk.

- You have written down your net worth, and you know how your assets are diversified.

- You know how you are spending your money and if you have a surplus for savings or a deficit.

There is one more step you can take that will help clarify your financial picture: Compare the categories in your financial plan with the whole picture.

For example, break down the categories of your expenses into percentages of your total expenses. These numbers will show you where you may be locked in financially, and where you may have more flexibility. Some people spend the biggest percentage of their income in taxes, others on housing—both fixed expenses with little room for flexibility. To find out how your spending patterns break down, in dollars and percentages, use the following worksheet. Once you list the dollar amount for each category, total the list. Then divide each amount by the total to derive the percentage. You can decide if my categories of fixed and discretionary expenses fit with your particular situation. If not, rearrange them to suit yourself.

MONTHLY   ANNUALLY

FIXED EXPENSES
Income taxes
FICA
Housing
  Mortgage/rent
  Repairs/upkeep
  Taxes
  Insurance
Food
  At home
  Meals out because of necessity
Insurance (life, disability)
Utilities
  Heating
  Water
  Electricity
  Telephone
Debts
Basic clothing (include outstanding bills)

MONTHLY   ANNUALLY

Personal necessities and services
(include outstanding bills)
Transportation
  Auto
  Insurance
  Loans
  Repairs
  Maintenance
  Fuel
  Public transportation
Medical/dental (cost after insurance)
Insurance

DISCRETIONARY EXPENSES
Travel
Gifts
More personal items and services
Impulse clothing
Entertainment and restaurants
Home improvements
Everything else you can think of (consult the list of discretionary
expenses you compiled to determine your cash flow)

This breakdown of your fixed and discretionary expenses can be very revealing. First compare the percentages
of your fixed expenses to your discretionary ones. If, for
example, your fixed expenses are 75 percent of your total
income, that probably means you are already on a very tight
budget. If the percentage ratio is 60 to 40, then you have more
leeway to spend on life-style, savings, and investment.

Now look at the individual percentages in both the fixed
and discretionary expenses category. If you find, for example, you are spending 30 percent of your income for
housing expenses, that seems reasonable. Much more than
that might mean you have very little left over for other fixed
expenses, even less for discretionary ones, and nothing for

savings. If the same is true of the percentages you find in your discretionary expenses or savings, you may want to cut down on these extras.

All of these percentages will show you *how* you spend your money, and you must decide if this pattern meets your intentions. If your goal is to increase your assets, you will see where you might cut back (or earn more) to get the surplus needed to get ahead in the money game. I recommend that your savings become a fixed expense every month, rather than a discretionary one, even if that means you have to cut back a little on other fixed expenses. Reconsider the amount of rent you are willing to pay, for example, or on discretionary expenses—those new clothes that you don't really need.

You can also apply this technique to focus on your asset and liability picture. Refer back to the list of assets you compiled in Chapter 5 and determine what percentage each category represents compared to your total. This will tell you, first of all, if the diversification of your assets meets your expectations for safety and growth. If 70 percent of your assets are in high-risk stocks, you may give that a second thought. Liquidity is a factor here, too. If 70 percent of your assets are in your home in the form of equity value, it means that amount of money is not readily available for savings, investment, or diversification. (The new home equity loans can give you some liquidity, but may be high-risk if they are made with variable interest rates. You could lose your home.) For some people, the purchase of a home with a large percentage of their assets may be appropriate. It may be the only way you can buy a home, or the way you feel safe. The point is not how you "should" allot your money, but to know if the percentages are appropriate to your risk level, your present situation, and your overall financial goals.

These percentage exercises are fairly simple but not

simplistic. They are an overview of your entire financial picture that permits you to see in perspective your strengths and weaknesses so you may make informed financial plans and follow up with decisions that reach your goals. Since your numbers will be changing, it is important to keep them relatively current. Financial pictures are of the moment only. I don't mean you need to become obsessed with numbers, to sit down every weekend to see how rich you are—moderation in all things. But the dynamics of creating your own plan will help you achieve your goals. It will be a great source of satisfaction that this success comes from your *own* efforts.

But how are you to achieve your financial goals? Do the investments you now own have the risk/reward relationship that is suitable for your situation? Which investments are likely to produce which results? What other investments should you consider? How does the spectrum of investments fit together in a pattern that you can understand?

Many women find putting all these numbers to work in a financial plan puzzling. But before we answer these questions, there are two more pieces to fit into the picture. They are subjects about which everyone talks as often as dieting and nutrition: taxes and inflation. Both require that you not only think in the language of numbers, but in a more sophisticated language: net numbers.

CHAPTER

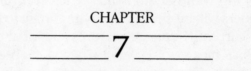

Alice in Wonderland

INFLATION AND TAXATION

WHEN most of us think about inflation, we remember the appealingly high interest rates on our bank accounts and money market funds of not so long ago. But we tend to forget how worried we all were when double-digit increases hit our bank loans, mortgages, and cost of living. Our earnings were not keeping up with the inflation rate, and it seemed to be undermining our future security. We never seemed able to get ahead.

This was particularly true for those whose money was mostly in some sort of savings vehicle. If, for example, your six-month certificate of deposit paid 12 percent, and at that time you were in a 33 percent tax bracket, you could figure that your *net* gain was 9 percent. Not quite. Because inflation was at 15 percent, you were *losing* money after taxes. So much for the good old days.

For the moment, at least, inflation has subsided, and we have a brand new tax code. But are we better off? Certainly the numbers are lower, and there are fewer of them.

TAX BRACKET SCHEDULE for individuals—2 rates: 15% or 28%

Filing single

taxable income up to	base tax		
$17,850 x 15% =	$2,678	+	28% of all income over $17,850

Filing jointly

taxable income up to	base tax		
$29,750 x 15% =	$4,463	+	28% of all income over $29,750

Filing head of household

taxable income up to	base tax		
$23,900 x 15% =	$3,585	+	28% of all income over $23,900

(1987 has some "blended rates" not included here)
EXCEPTIONS, which mean you can pay more:

1. There's a surcharge of 5 percent for married couples with taxable income over $71,900, or for singles over $43,150, which works to phase out the 15 percent and personal exemption benefits.

2. There's a flat rate of 28 percent on all income (no 15 percent category), which applies to married couples with income over $149,250, or to singles with income over $89,560.

The old tax game was called "Avoidance," and that meant borrowing now to pay off in tomorrow's cheaper dollars while "writing off" the interest. Conservative investors, many women among them, sought tax-free municipal bonds and tax-favored capital gains vehicles such as real estate. Higher-risk investors bought highly leveraged real estate "deals" or energy and research/development partnerships, which provided special tax privileges. The language and concepts of tax sheltering were all very complicated and esoteric. But it did give the male "club" something besides sports to talk about over the water cooler at work, at dinner parties, and on the golf course. Do you remember "phantom income," "alternative minimum tax," "depletion allowances," and losses as bonuses?

Now it is all upside down. Deflation and tax law changes make the opposite true. Borrowing or leverage can be dangerous when interest rates and values are falling. Losses are now losses. And giving up liquidity for long-term tax deferrals isn't necessarily desirable.

A wide range of investments, especially liquid financial instruments, are more appealing now that the rules have changed and net return is calculated differently. But *thinking net* is still a valid concept: what you keep—after tax and after inflation.

HOW TO DETERMINE YOUR TAXABLE INCOME TO FIND YOUR BRACKET

Here's a simplified recipe (consult your accountant for specifics that apply to you).

Add: *Income* (wages, commissions, interest, dividends, capital gains, rents, unemployment compensation, other) to get your *gross income*.

Subtract: *adjustments* (per new limitations: IRA/KEOGH, business expenses, others) to get your *adjusted gross income.*

Subtract: *itemized deductions* (per new limitations: medical, state and local taxes, mortgage interest, charitable contributions, miscellaneous deductions).

Subtract: *personal exemptions.* Now you're left with your *taxable income.* Look this figure up on the tax table to find your bracket percentage.

To find your tax liability:

Get your *tax* from the table.

Add surcharge for phase-out of 15 percent rate.

Add surcharge for phase-out of personal exemption.

Subtract tax credits (apply alternative minimum tax if applicable); this gives you your *tax liability*.

Subtract *prepayments;* you're left with your *net tax due or refund*.

THE DETAILS

PERSONAL EXEMPTION	$2,000 ($1,950 in 1988) phased out for incomes above $149,250.
STANDARD DEDUCTION	$5,000 (joint) $4,400 (head of household) $3,000 (single)
OTHER DEDUCTIONS	
Mortgage interest	Principal and second residence up to purchase cost plus improvements. Home equity loans only for special cause: medical, education, home purchase.
Investment interest (includes rents)	Up to amount equal to investment income (phased in). No consumer interest. No loss from passive income-partnerships and other nonactive business interests to offset other income (some exceptions).
Charitable contributions	For itemizers.
State and local taxes	But not sales tax.

Long-term and short-term capital gains	28% top rate. No difference from ordinary income.
Individual Retirement Accounts	$2,000 deductible only if Adjusted Gross Income is below $40,000 (joint) or $25,000 (single) and if not covered by employer plan. Spousal IRA of $250 is allowed. Some partial deductions for incomes between $40,000 and $50,000 (joint) and $25,000 and $35,000 (single). Interest and appreciation not taxable inside the IRA.
401(K) Tax-deferred savings plans	$7,000 deductible limit.
Medical expenses	Only if in excess of 7.5% of Adjusted Gross Income.
Miscellaneous (such as business and investment expenses)	Only if in excess of 2% of Adjusted Gross Income.

OTHER CHANGES

Not all newer-issued municipal bonds are tax-free—be sure of what you buy.

Add special credits for child or elderly care, low incomes, investments in low-income housing.

Transferring of income to children to avoid taxes doesn't work if the income exceeds $1,000. It will be taxed in the parents' bracket, and the children will need Social Security numbers.

Dividend exclusion, working-marrieds deduction, and income averaging are no longer permitted.

Business meals and entertainment deductions are limited to 80 percent within the miscellaneous limitation provision.

Investment real estate has new depreciation allowances, all "straight-line" (every year is the same): 27½ years for residentials, 31½ years for commercial.

Fellowships, scholarships, and unemployment benefits are taxed.

Oil and gas investments have some special exemptions.

"Alternative minimum tax" rules are tougher—more preference items, thus ensuring that the rich pay more in tax.

You should now know your tax bracket percentage. Bracket means the amount you pay on your last dollar, not a percentage of all income (unless you qualify for high-income treatment). You probably guessed your bracket, since the choice is much easier than it used to be—only two. You can now apply this knowledge to investment decisions. For instance, if you have $10,000 to invest and are trying to decide between a taxable bank account or a tax-free municipal bond, *and* you are in the 28 percent federal tax bracket, you would calculate the following:

Insured Bank CD–10 years		*AAA Municipal Bond–10 years*	
Interest rate	9%	Interest rate	7%
Interest	$900	Interest	$700
Tax (28%)	$242	Tax	$–0–
Net return	$648	Net return	$700

The municipal bond gives you a better return. Since municipal bonds may also be free of state tax (if you own a bond from a municipal issuer in your home state), you may come out even better. Depending on your state's tax code, your actual tax bracket may be higher than indicated in this calculation of the federal bracket, and the benefit of tax-free income may be more.

Next, compare this rate of return with the inflation rate. To be fair, it should be compared with what you might guess will be the average inflation over the same time period as the investment, ten years. If, for example, you expect inflation to average 8 percent over the next ten years, both the insured (taxable) bank CD at 9 percent and the AAA municipal bond at 7 percent will fall slightly behind.

These two income-reducers—taxes and inflation—will never disappear and will probably not remain at current rates. So don't get too comfortable and *always* take them into consideration with every investment decision.

Many of my clients refused to consider longer-term income investments when interest rates were high. Why? Because they thought they would go higher. Everyone was scurrying around, looking for inflation-sensitive investments. When inflation began to ease, it didn't make believers out of people right away. Gasoline prices and mortgage rates were falling, which was pleasing. But many investors failed to see or accept the other half of the picture, that interest rates fell, too. In any financial climate, it is hard to erase the recent past and to think in a new scenario. In fact, many people waited too long.

Sophie and Sam Sunbelt are retirees who live in Florida in a home they own outright. Wanting to retain control over their assets, the Sunbelts invest only in six- to twelve-month CDs. In the early 1980s, these were paying close to 15 percent interest, allowing Sophie and Sam to expand their life-style to include some unexpected luxuries. The trouble is they began to think of the luxuries as necessities. Interest rates have since declined into the single digits, and their income from the CDs is considerably less. But the Sunbelts haven't reduced their life-style accordingly. The result?

They're dipping into capital. People often "lock in" their money for a longer time to get higher interest rates *after* interest rates have gone down.

Sophie and Sam might react the way many people do. They go for the investment with the highest advertised yield. They no longer pay attention to exactly what they are buying. They forget to note the length of time, being mesmerized by the idea of "tax-free." They have never bought a twenty-year CD in their lives, yet are willing to tie their money into a twenty-year portfolio of tax-free bonds.

Or they might go for one of these government funds that a broker told them about on the phone. They don't know that this fund has no specified maturity, but twelve to thirty years is probable. The return will fluctuate, and the fund hedges and speculates with options to increase the yield. They also have failed to notice that the major aim of the fund is "current cash return," which sounds good, but could also mean the sacrifice of some principal if they liquidate early.

The Sunbelts also see ads for "high-yield funds" that have better rates. What they don't know is that this phrase is financial jargon for a portfolio of lower-quality bonds. Before this, Sam always said he would only invest in insured CDs similar to AAA bonds.

The Sunbelts aren't alone in trying to recapture inflation-era yields in a less inflationary period, and they are not alone in thinking short-term because of their age. In times of dramatic change, the promoters and gurus bombard the financial press so as to take advantage of the panic. A big problem in making investment plans is not knowing what the future economic trend will be. Volatility is hard to live with when making investment decisions. Some investments are better suited for an inflationary environment than others. Some investments make more sense if they are bought on the basis of earnings and cash flow rather than on tax protection. When the game changes suddenly, investment strategies fail.

STRATEGIES FOR GETTING AHEAD

There are several strategies that will maximize your chances of success in your investment plan.

Relate to your personal circumstances first. For example, Sophie and Sam need cash flow now, yet they cannot afford any risk to their capital. Their advanced age is a controlling factor in their investment strategy. Here is an abbreviated summary of their financial situation:

Income-producing assets:	$100,000

Income:	
Joint Social Security income	11,000
Sam's pension	6,000
Investment income at current rate of 6%	6,000
Total	$ 23,000
Outgo:	$ 25,500

Deficit!

Their investment strategy: To compromise some on life-style in order to conserve principal and to extend maturities on their investments *moderately* in order to increase yield.

In my opinion (and contrary to much financial advice I read), it would not be wise for Sam and Sophie to invest in long-term portfolios. The slightly greater yield does not warrant the exposure of the portfolio should inflation return while they live to a now-common older age. Inflation could decimate their income. Long-term, fixed-income investments get hurt during rising inflation. Furthermore, I would recommend the highest-quality investments for those assets that cannot be risked at all just in case the economy deflates further, which would put certain debt investments at risk. I would "bet" on Sam and Sophie living on, with time to make new decisions as the investment cycle and interest rates change. Moderately longer maturities keep their options open.

Pay attention to trends. Finance, like fashion, runs in cycles. Change is a given condition of both. To keep up, you have to read the magazines, newspapers, and regard what hints the media are giving about changes and trends. World news and economic news count, too. Political events often reflect economic circumstances. International trade legislation affects the cost of your new Mercedes and Italian fashion shoes, and maybe whether you can afford to buy them at all. As an investment adviser, I have had to learn to "read between the lines," to make estimates of what to expect. We all have to pay attention. The effects of the tax law changes for real estate, for example, could be inferred long before the legislation was passed or the exact terms known. The mood of the public and then Congress toward tax avoidance was quite clear.

Diversify. Diversification of your assets can be a hedge if you don't know which way the economy will crumble. A diversified portfolio could include some real estate, some stocks, some bonds, and some bank accounts—depending on your unique situation. You could also diversify within one investment choice, such as CDs or government bonds with *sequential maturities.* That way, you "average up or down" as interest rates change and investments mature. Good for those of you who don't want to make predictions and worry—you can just play bridge and forget it. In any case, it is rarely a good strategy to have most of your assets in a single investment.

Think net. If you are saving and investing for a future goal, how do you calculate your "real" return? How much meat is left after the butcher trims the fat and removes the bone? It depends on whether your price per pound is before trimming or after!

As discussed in comparing taxable and nontaxable investments, always regard an investment return on its *after-tax* basis and always consider an investment return on an *after-inflation* basis. If your after-tax return is 5 percent and inflation is at 4 percent, you are ahead, net-net, 1 percent! Don't put it down; you can't always make big bucks with all of your investment money. At least you are *safely* "treading water" until a better opportunity presents itself.

Consider the effects of compounding. Compounding is money earning interest, then the money plus the interest earning more interest, and so forth. It is money "making" money.

Compound interest charts reveal how your money grows, and I've included a simplified one in Fig. 7–1. In reverse, it shows what your money would be worth with any assumed inflation rate. The left-hand column represents the number of years you are considering. The percentages represent the interest you are receiving or the rate of inflation you predict.

If you are worried about the value of your assets within an inflation scenario, this chart will give you numbers to worry with. For the inflation calculation, each number is the factor you *divide* into your principal. If you wish to estimate an average inflation rate of 7 percent over the next ten years, an asset of $10,000 will be worth approximately $5,076 in today's dollars ($10,000 divided by 1.97 equals $5,076).

Or if you wish to think positive and calculate how your money will grow in a certain number of years, use the

Fig. 7–1 *Annual Compound Interest and Inflation Chart*

Years	4%	6%	7%	10%
1	1.04	1.06	1.07	1.10
2	1.08	1.12	1.14	1.21
3	1.12	1.19	1.23	1.33
4	1.16	1.26	1.31	1.46
5	1.22	1.34	1.40	1.61
10	1.48	1.79	1.97	2.59
15	1.80	2.40	2.76	4.18
30	3.24	5.74	7.61	17.45

compound interest calculation. *Multiply* your capital figure by the appropriate factor for the number of years of saving. Interest of 7 percent over ten years will make your $10,000 worth $19,700 ($10,000 multiplied by 1.97 equals $19,700).

As the chart indicates, compound interest and compound inflation are mirror images. If the interest rate (after taxes) is the same as the inflation rate, you are just even. You make 7 percent interest, you lose 7 percent buying power.

The Rule of 72. There is a quick way to estimate the time in which your money will double in value from compounding or be worth half from inflation. It is called the Rule of 72—one of those mystical mathematical wonders that you might find useful when you are not carrying your compound interest chart in your purse.

To make the calculation, divide 72 by your estimated rate of inflation to find the number of years it will take for your money to be worth half its present value. For example, take $100,000 that is not earning any interest for this example. Assume a modest inflation rate of 3 percent. If that rate continues, it will take approximately twenty-four years for your asset to be worth only half its present value (72 divided by 3 equals 24).

But if the inflation rate is averaging 8 percent (which has been more typical), then it will only take about nine years. In nine years your $100,000 will buy just $50,000 of today's dollars' worth of goods and services.

With these time frames in mind, you can begin to see why being aware of both present and possible future inflation rates is important to your investing strategy. It's as if the speed of a "down" escalator were changed from "low" to "high"; it's the way it is when my three grown sons come home to visit: They eat it quicker than I can buy and cook it!

Of course, ordinarily you would be earning interest on such an asset. And this is just the point, and why the Rule of 72 is useful: To calculate what it takes to offset inflation, you must earn after tax at least at the inflation rate.

You can also use the Rule of 72 to calculate compound interest. Divide 72 by the rate of interest to find the number of years for your money to double. If you invest $100,000 at 8 percent, it will take about nine years to be worth $200,000 (72 divided by 8 equals 9).

INVESTING A LUMP-SUM ASSET

Common ways in which women acquire large, lump-sum assets are through divorce, sale of a residence, or inheritance. In many cases, after paying taxes and living expenses, this lump-sum asset may be the only major savings for the future. That much money is hard to come by, and it should be invested wisely.

Princess Perfect was married to Mr. White Knight for twenty-five years. They lived in a suburban dream home in

Happy Valley, belonged to the country club, and would retire on his corporate pension. Their net worth was $320,000. Princess earns $25,000 as a teacher, a far cry from White's $75,000.

Then the unexpected: They divorced.

She receives about half their net worth, $160,000, most of it in cash from the sale of the house. She also gets $20,000 a year alimony for three years. Her financial picture looks like this:

$100,000 into a condo

  20,000 cash, into the bank for emergencies

   5,000 stays in her IRA compounding tax-deferred

  25,000 her teacher's annuity, for retirement

  10,000 investment capital, into stocks

She keeps her car (Mr. Knight pays off the loan) and most of the household stuff. All his life insurance is assigned to the kids.

Princess is safe in her tower condo. She and her ex-husband have about the same assets to start with, but different income potential. Her life-style will be different from his simply because wealth comes in two forms: assets and income. His cash flow continues undiminished. The Dragon Inflation will be more difficult for Ms. Perfect without Mr. White Knight once the alimony stops. She doesn't have enough assets or income for the high life-style she envisioned for her later years. But she has a home and a pension, and her life-style, though reduced, is probably secure.

In contrast is the situation of Denise Deskbound. Aged sixty-one, divorced in her later years, Denise is working as a secretary for $17,000 a year. She has $30,000, a lump-sum settlement from her ex, plus an IRA with another $8,000.

Denise doesn't like her work and wonders how much longer she can do it. Next year she would qualify for Social Security, but she expects to receive only $450 a month. Her rent alone is $475, and going up. She lives in Los Angeles, an expensive housing market. Her children cannot help her.

What should Denise do?

Women worry about this typical predicament. Work, especially in the pink-collar ghetto, becomes more difficult with age, and it is harder to be hired. Inflation, even if modest, is likely to push up Denise's rent. She cannot afford to buy a home in the area, and her $30,000 prevents her from qualifying for public housing assistance.

I have no investment to suggest that could increase Denise's income significantly. In fact, since this is all she has, she cannot afford any risk, and must settle for moderate yields. I recommend that she consider moving to a community where condominiums or small houses can be found for $50,000 or $60,000. With a $30,000 down payment, she could afford the mortgage, insurance, and taxes, all of which would be less than current rent. Her IRA money becomes the emergency savings fund, and since she is over age 59½, she can use it without penalty—and should continue to fund it for tax-deferred compounding even without the deduction of former years.

Owning a home with a fixed mortgage rate is a way to "fix" our largest living expense. It is also a way to increase a woman's security. The cost of the house and payments on the mortgage may be relatively less than the cost of future inflation. I also encouraged Denise to continue working as long as possible. Finding a renter to share her expenses is a possibility, too, if she finds a two-bedroom home. In another community, her wages might be lower, forcing her to be more frugal, which will be difficult. If she enacts this plan, she may be all right. If not, as she ages, and expenses and inflation eat away at her savings, she will need public assistance.

SAVING AS YOU GO

Not all women have a lump-sum asset to invest. But if you are salaried, or have some other regular source of income, you can build your assets by putting specified amounts into savings on a regular basis. I have included Fig. 7–2 to show how much a monthly addition of $100 to savings will be worth, including compound interest of varying rates, at the end of specified periods of time.

Fig. 7–2   Savings Chart per $100

Year	5%	7%	10%
1	$ 1,222	$ 1,239	$ 1,256
2	2,494	2,568	2,645
3	3,818	3,993	4,178
4	5,196	5,520	5,872
5	6,629	7,159	7,743
10	14,725	17,308	20,484
15	24,609	31,696	41,447
30	69,405	121,997	226,048

As stated, this chart assumes a savings of $100 per month, but you can adjust that number easily to the amount you wish to save as a percentage of $100. For example, if you are going to save $50 a month, decrease all numbers by 50 percent. So $50 per month saved at 7 percent for ten years would become $8,654 (half of $17,308). The chart in Fig. 7–2 does not reflect tax consequences. So, when choosing

a compounding rate, remember to consider it on the basis
of your after-tax rate of interest.

PUTTING IT ALL TOGETHER

Now that you know how they work, you can use both
charts—compounding a lump sum and savings as you go—
to assess your present—and future—financial situation.
These calculations are especially useful in planning for your
retirement regardless of whether your target date is three
or thirty years from now. To figure out how it works you
need to:

Decide *when* you wish to retire—number of years from
now.

Decide the annual *income* you will need—in today's dollars.

Find your investment *net worth* as shown in this book.

Know your cash flow and *savings* ability as shown in this
book.

Find out your expected retirement income from pensions
or Social Security. It is available upon request.

Estimate an interest rate for your investment return.

Estimate an inflation average for the time period (interest
rates and inflation are tied together, so if you estimate in the
wrong direction on both, actual rates should cancel out your
error).

Nancy Nurturer, a fifty-two-year-old social worker, expects to retire in ten years. She would like an annual
income of $20,000 in today's dollars. How can she succeed?
Nancy has investment capital of $25,000. She assumes an
after-tax return of 7 percent, her assets compound 1.97
times in ten years to $49,250. If that sum earned 7 percent
she could expect annual income of:

$3,447.50

Next she takes her monthly savings figure, $100 at 7 percent. The chart indicates that figure would grow to $17,308. Again, if this sum earns 7 percent, she will have additional annual income of:

$1,211.56

To this she adds her annual pension expectations:

$ 12,000.00

Total $16,659.06

So far so good, but Nancy hasn't considered inflation. She guesses inflation to average 6 percent over the same time period. Using the compound interest chart, she must adjust the $16,650 to $9,300 in today's dollars ($16,659.06 divided by 1.79 equals $9,306.74).

Fortunately, she has another source of income, Social Security. She expects $550 a month, or annualized: $6,600. She does not adjust this for inflation because it will be factored in if regulations remain the same. Therefore, her *total retirement income* will be $15,906.74.

Nancy does not meet her goal. If she is dissatisfied, she must reassess her priorities, her expectations, or both. Of course, yields and inflation will change in real time, as might her (or your) savings ability; but calculations like this give you an idea of the possibility or improbability of achieving your goal. Annual monitoring will tell you if you are on target (particularly with your estimates of interest rates and inflation). The numbers give the answers. Believe them. Use them.

TAX HINTS FOR THE ASSERTIVE WOMAN

What measures can you consider to reduce your taxes under the current law? There are fewer gimmicks, but take what you are legally entitled to.

1. Consider using any pension plans available to you. IRA deductions are still available to workers not covered by another pension plan. In any case, the interest earned is tax-deferred until you take the money out so it may make sense for you anyway. KEOGH plans for self-employed people have been restricted to $7,000, but they are still available.

2. Insurance and annuity programs are still tax-advantaged. Cash values in insurance policies are not taxed, and neither are the proceeds from life insurance. Annuities still provide tax-deferred compounding of the investment until the money is removed. Watch for tax law changes here.

3. Use all the deductions available to you. These are described earlier in this chapter with the details on how to figure your taxable income.

The mortgage on your home (or second home) is still deductible. Improvements to the property will increase your cost basis, making the sale price less taxable.

Be careful of those nonmortgage loans from relatives, which don't count as mortgages. Consumer loans, which these would be, are no longer deductible. It doesn't make sense to finance cars and credit cards. It probably never did, unless you didn't have any other way to buy these things or made more money with the liquidity.

Many real estate investments need to be reconsidered without the tremendous leverage that was once characteristic. Run the numbers and look for positive cash flow. Remember when we all knew instinctively not to invest unless we made money?

In sum, inflation and taxation both affect your investment bottom line. To formulate your own financial plan, once you get past the hard facts (your goals, your net worth, your cash flow), it becomes necessary to make some reasonable estimates about inflation and taxation. Like anything in the real world, these numbers will change. Investment performance in varying economic climates is also an unknown, but rough numbers, and revisions as you go, will help. Financial plans are outlines, not promises that can't be broken. Circumstances may change the shape of the plan, or assertive action may make it work even better. This is why doing your own financial planning is important; you will have the best feel for your own circumstances and risk-tolerance level.

The experts don't know the future any better than you do, and there is no "science" to predictions. It is true that some people seem to have a talent for making money, and their own luck, but training and discipline fit in there somewhere. Investment opportunities come along for those who pay attention and are in control of their own affairs.

CHAPTER

I Have This Money; What Should I Do with It?

INVESTING FOR INCOME AND SAFETY

Put it in the bank?

Ask my accountant?

Hide it from the IRS?

Buy stocks my boyfriend recommends?

Buy a government-guaranteed fund with the highest advertised yield?

Ask a male family friend to act as my adviser?

Buy a house?

Go to a financial planner who sells limited partnerships?

Buy a "high-yield" fund?

Take a trip around the world?

Buy gold?

Hire a money manager?

Set up a trust at a bank and let them take care of it?

Buy a tax-free fund with the highest advertised yield?

Give a party?

Ask my attorney?

Buy second mortgages?

Find a broker who specializes in women on their own?

Find a financial planner who sells insurance?

Buy U.S. EE bonds?

Quit work?

Lend it to my kids?

Put it in a numbered Swiss bank account?

Find a broker who is an expert in options?

Put it in my money market fund?

Fund a risk venture to develop a new product?

Pay off debts?

Go to Atlantic City?

Once I decide, do it, and forget about it?

Other ideas?

Thinking about the kinds of questions, such as these, that women at seminars and in my office ask me, I realized that something very basic was missing in the average woman's perception of the financial world. Remembering my own lack of understanding, I believe that, somewhere along the way, no one has bothered to explain it all to us in an organized context. With this understanding (plus the knowledge of your own financial needs), you can develop an appropriate financial plan, and the answer to "What should I do with this money?" will be clearer.

Few of us can escape some information about money, with financial news now all over the TV as well as in print. Money talk is in vogue. Knowing the way it all fits together makes sense out of the information. This includes risk/reward assessment, how different investments react during financial cycles, and how the marketplace works. By knowing how to think about types of investments generally, you can look at a specific investment and separate the facts from the hype.

I am big on organizing things; I am a closet cleaner. It is easy to understand the investment world if you see it as a spectrum of choices in a certain, purposeful order, with categories of similar characteristics. You know: The office clothes all go together, and the weekend and party clothes each have their own space. By devising a frame of reference for investments, you can classify each in a place of its own so that it will be meaningful. Then you will be able to evaluate unfamiliar investments by their characteristics as they relate to this frame of reference.

The other problem women often face in the investment world is vocabulary—street jargon. Every industry has its own vocabulary. Jargon can be a helpful shorthand, but it can also be used like a secret password or handshake to prove that the speaker is a member of the club. And it can be used to impress, rather than clarify. Since women are latecomers to the Financial Club, I will make a point of using the jargon of Wall Street in context, so the terms can become part of your vocabulary. I have included a glossary of important financial terms at the back of this book, but you will read or hear many more words that require further research or explanation.

JOINING THE CLUB

To devise a financial frame of reference, think about investments in three basic categories, each with different objectives:

Investments that conserve wealth—usually by producing income at very low risk.

Investments that grow internally and increase wealth—usually with increased risk.

Speculations aiming for dramatic profits—high-risk long-shots.

I place all investments in a triangle, according to what I consider their degree of risk (Fig. 8–1).

Fig. 8–1   Investment Triangle

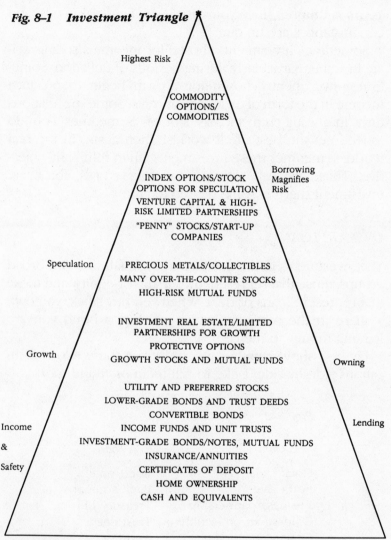

Highest Risk

COMMODITY
OPTIONS/
COMMODITIES

INDEX OPTIONS/STOCK
OPTIONS FOR SPECULATION

Borrowing
Magnifies
Risk

VENTURE CAPITAL & HIGH-
RISK LIMITED PARTNERSHIPS

"PENNY" STOCKS/START-UP
COMPANIES

Speculation

PRECIOUS METALS/COLLECTIBLES
MANY OVER-THE-COUNTER STOCKS
HIGH-RISK MUTUAL FUNDS

INVESTMENT REAL ESTATE/LIMITED
PARTNERSHIPS FOR GROWTH
PROTECTIVE OPTIONS

Growth

GROWTH STOCKS AND MUTUAL FUNDS

Owning

UTILITY AND PREFERRED STOCKS
LOWER-GRADE BONDS AND TRUST DEEDS
CONVERTIBLE BONDS

Income

INCOME FUNDS AND UNIT TRUSTS

Lending

&

INVESTMENT-GRADE BONDS/NOTES, MUTUAL FUNDS
INSURANCE/ANNUITIES

Safety

CERTIFICATES OF DEPOSIT
HOME OWNERSHIP
CASH AND EQUIVALENTS

Lowest Risk

The placement of the spectrum of investments in these
categories is debatable, especially since market conditions
change notions of what is safe and what is wise. But think of
this financial frame of reference as generally true. There is
no ideal investment triangle; each of us will have our own.

Yours is unique, since your risk level, financial needs, and circumstances are unique.

Sometimes investments chosen for income also appreciate in value, particularly during periods of deflation. Sometimes investments chosen for growth begin to produce income in the form of dividends or rents. Some speculations turn into blue-chip success stories. Sometimes you do indeed get the best of all worlds! Then again, in the real world, sometimes these investments fail to fulfill any objective. These we call "losers." In other words, for every investment there is some degree of risk.

OWN OR LOAN?

The investments in the financial triangle fall into two broad groups: those that represent ownership or equity, and those that represent loans or debt. When you buy stock, you own a share in the company; when you buy a bond you are loaning money to the company.

Fig. 8–2 shows another way to look at these two classifications side by side. I like to call them *own* and *loan*.

Fig. 8–2

You *Own*	You *Loan*
Stock	Bond/note
Real estate	Bank account
Business/partnership	Treasury bill
Gold/silver/collectible	Trust deed
Option/commodity	Annuity

Notice that the low-risk or conservative section of the investment triangle consists mostly of *debt* instruments and the growth section upward consists mostly of *equity* instruments. Ownership of growth securities usually entails more risk—and more potential for reward.

INVESTING TO CONSERVE ASSETS

Most investors have a greater percentage of their assets in the conservative section of the investment triangle in the form of home ownership, savings, retirement funds, and insurance. Home ownership is usually categorized as conservative even though it tends to increase in value. This is so because it serves as more than an equity-building profit center: You live there. Insurance is also considered conservative: It protects the value of your assets or income stream in case of adversity. And don't forget that as your net worth increases, so do your liabilities. Many women who have struggled to get ahead forget that once they do, they have something to protect. People sue those with assets. Annuities are investment vehicles for retirement funds, generally regarded as conservative because their principal is protected (though not necessarily guaranteed) by insurance companies. And, finally, cash and its equivalents (checking and savings accounts, bank CDs, money market funds, etc.) are considered conservative because they are totally liquid: You can get your hands on them immediately.

Speaking of cash-on-hand, I once read about a woman who saved all her wages in the pocket of an old pink bathrobe that she hung on a hook in her employer's garage. Her financial goal was to save enough money to take a trip home to see her relatives. The employer had a garage sale and sold her robe for $1.

U.S. Treasury bills, which are easily salable, can also be considered a cash equivalent. The "riskless" rate of return (as it usually is thought of) on T-bills is often the standard that other investment choices are measured against, to determine if the risk is worth it.

BONDS

Moving up the investment triangle, consider the income producing investment: bonds.

Just the word *bond* sounds banker-gray and dull. But bear with me through this explanation, because if you understand how bonds work, how they are priced in the marketplace, you will understand why interest rates are such an important topic of conversation in the financial news, what the hullabaloo is all about, and why every woman who wants to invest should know about them. It is essential that you understand the concepts behind these debt instruments because they connect with all other investments in the financial world. All investments compete for money in the marketplace—not much different from the competition for your consumer dollar, which we women understand very well.

There are many different kinds of bonds, but basically they all work the same way. A bond is actually a contract in which you agree to lend the issuer of the bond your money for a specified rate of interest for a specified period of time. You are paid that interest for the specified period of time, then your "principal" is returned, and the deal is over.

If you own a U.S. Treasury bond (note or bill), which is state tax–free, you are lending your money to the U.S. government and you own part of the national debt. You can also lend your money to an entity of the state or local government, which issues municipal bonds with interest payments that are for the most part federally and in some cases state tax–free. Or you can lend your money to private corporations that issue corporate bonds paying interest that is fully taxable. There are many variations of the terms of bonds, mostly to do with variable rates, when the interest is paid, or when the contract might be interrupted early. These variations are described in the glossary at the end of the book.

HOW THE MARKETPLACE FOR BONDS WORKS

Economic conditions, like soap operas, are always in a state of change, and these changes influence the value of the bonds.

Suppose your broker calls you to tell you of a new bond offering, coming to market at *face* or *par* value of $1,000. (Normally, most bonds are offered in $5,000 amounts, but let's keep it simple.) Since your money is a valuable commodity, the borrower will compensate you at the going rate, or *coupon,* of 10 percent. This coupon means $100 a year in *interest.* When the bond *matures* on its due date, you will get back your original investment (the principal) in full.

$1,000 E.Z. Corporation bond
offered at 100% of par (called "100")
10% due 6/1/01
Value: $1,000

You buy it.
The next month you get a statement from your broker that looks like this:

$1,000 E.Z. Corporation
10% due 6/1/01
Quoted price: 90
Value: $900

"Wait a minute! I just lost $100! I didn't invest conservatively to lose money!" Grabbing the telephone, you put the question to your broker, "What happened?"

Your friendly broker explains: It so happens that right now interest rates for similar bonds are higher. Why should that affect your bond? If the competition is paying 11.4 percent, who would buy your bond at 10 percent? (Your brokerage statement assumes the sell price or bid.) Nobody, unless you lower the price of your bond—discount it—so that your effective yield is the same as the competition's.

The market value of bonds is inverse to interest rates. When interest rates go up, market value goes down, and your bonds would sell at a discount. But the reverse is also true: If interest rates fall, the value of your bond increases to a premium and would then sell above par, or above the amount it will be worth at maturity.

Since all investments are measured against each other, serious investors are comparison shoppers, moving money to the best advantage. During periods of inflation, for example, interest rates rise because the cost of borrowing money is increasing. When interest rates seem to be "topping out," investors may turn to bonds with their guaranteed rates of return rather than risk ownership in stocks, which carry no such guarantee. If an investor buys a bond when interest rates are high and then they fall, her bonds will be more valuable. She can make a profit on the sale price in addition to the generous interest rate. Such profits are now taxed at the same rate as other income even if they are still referred to as "capital gains."

Issuing bonds is a way to borrow money, which the issuer must repay out of earnings or receipts. Inflation can be hard on corporate cash flow. This means that the stocks of corporations carrying too large a debt may not do well. But there are some other considerations, such as interest rates (the cost of money) and tax benefits to corporate interest payments on debt. Firms may consider these factors when deciding whether to issue debt instruments (bonds) or equity instruments (stocks).

On the other hand, the assets of companies in some fields—real estate, energy, and natural resources, for example—often grow with inflation. The temptation in this situation is to meet the demand for their products or services by heavy borrowing, meaning they issue bonds with high coupon rates. Guess what happens when deflation sets in? Trouble, such as the oil and gas companies have experienced in the recent past. Income falls, but they must still pay the high coupon rates to their bondholders. Investment behavior ties all these factors together, along with economic assessments by those who manage their money well.

A well-off, nonworking woman in her middle years came to me to learn what tax-free municipal bonds were and how to determine their value. It seems that her aged father, who supported her, bought nonregistered municipal bonds so that he could keep his wealth a secret. (Municipal issues must now be registered, but older issues with nonregistered "coupons" can still be bought in the secondary marketplace.) Apparently, the secrecy factor was more important to the father than investment considerations. Furthermore, the daughter did not know where he kept the bonds—and her father's health was failing. Although she had seen many trade confirmations, he refused to tell her anything. There is no way to determine value without exact information as to the amount and security description. She needed the bonds or his records to determine their worth. Clearly, she was worried as to the suitability of his investment portfolio for the remainder of his years—and concerned with her own inheritance. Since the woman never came back, I don't know what finally happened (did she

ever find out where the bonds were?), and I can't say if this
tale ended happily ever after.

HOW BOND VALUES ARE MEASURED

The value of a bond is called its yield, and there are several
yields to be aware of:

The *coupon yield* is the percentage of $1,000, or par
value of the bond, promised to the investor in the contract.

The *current yield* is the one you would be most likely to
figure out for yourself. It is the direct ratio of cash received
in interest to cash spent buying the bond—called "cash on
cash." It is the same as the coupon yield only if the bond is
bought at par. If you receive $100 per year in interest, but
bought the bond at a discount of $900, your current yield is
11 percent ($100 divided by $900).

The *yield to maturity* accounts for the current yield plus
the difference, whether profit or loss, between purchase
price and maturity price. In our example, a bond purchased
at $900 receives $100 per year in interest and on maturity
you would profit by another $100 since $1,000 would be
returned to you. This is a yield to maturity of 11.4 percent.
This is not a simple calculation; I looked it up in a bond
table. Bond traders use specialized calculators that account
for every day of interest due.

Most bonds are quoted and compared on the basis of
yield to maturity. Since that figure includes all the relevant
factors, it is the most correct. It is called "the basis." Only
bonds that have no definite due date—such as Government
National Mortgage Association bonds (GNMAs), "Ginnie
Maes"—are quoted on current yield. So you cannot compare them to standard bonds when deciding on a purchase.
Their yield to maturity is unknown, since mortgage payoffs
occur unpredictably—and will probably turn out considerably different than the current yield indicates. Most GNMA
funds are bought at a premium in order to advertise a high

current yield. In the end, their yield will be lower, since the principal you receive will be less than you paid.

Many women investors reveal their vulnerability by na-ively mixing up the words *dividends* and *interest, stocks* and *bonds.* They are not the same thing. So please remember: *interest goes with bonds, dividends go with stocks.*

If you understand so far, you've got it! You are now a relatively knowledgeable woman investor. The rest follows logically.

The longer the risk, the higher the yield. The longer you hold a bond, the greater the risk to your principal. So as a good businesswoman, you charge more interest. And if a bond is close to maturity, the risk is reduced—even if it was originally assigned a low rating. Ratings don't change as bonds get closer to maturity, but they should be considered safer. A lower-rated bond may represent good value as it comes closer to maturity.

The lower the quality, the higher the yield. All bonds, like meat in the grocery store, are graded as to quality (AAA, AA, A, BAA). Buy a lower-grade bond, expect more compensa-tion. Buy a lower-grade of beef, get more of it for your dollar.

The conservative portion of the investment triangle also includes other interest-sensitive instruments. Funds and unit trusts, of course, are just "bundled" securities. They are a convenient way to buy a diversified portfolio of bonds or other securities. Investments that focus on income, even if they happen to be called stocks—indicating ownership—or bank accounts, mortgages, or others, compete with each other and tend to behave in the same way with regard to interest rates. So a utility stock, which pays out its earnings in dividends, acts more like a bond in its market valuation. That is why the prices of utility stocks reached new highs as interest rates went down—not necessarily because they were making great profits. *When interest rates are falling, interest-sensitive investments generally increase in value.*

You can now consider yourself a sophisticated woman investor!

CHAPTER

9

Up the Triangle

INVESTING FOR GROWTH
AND TIPS ON RECORD KEEPING

MOVING up the investment triangle, we come to the focus of attention of the "bull market" (note the gender of this phenomenon): stocks. When stocks are increasing in value, investors rush to buy. Great percentage gains make it seem like "easy money." Mutual funds become popular because even the unsophisticated buyer has a chance at diversification, professional management, and smaller unit purchases. Rumors of corporate "buyouts" at inflated prices are in constant circulation. It all seems so tempting—investors pour money into the stock market in the hopes of making more money. When interest rates drop dramatically, fixed-income investments don't appear as attractive; they are less competitive. Money tends to move toward stocks; risk-taking may be more worthwhile. This is especially true if the investment is in stocks that benefit from lower borrowing costs. The mid-1986 "bull market" exploded because of lower interest rates, IRA and other pension investments, and, finally, from tax law changes that made liquid, financial instruments more competitive with real estate.

Owning stock is like marriage. You are not guaranteed a dividend or salary (and you may have to clean and cook), but as a partner, you get a piece of the action. You participate in its fortunes or misfortunes. However, divorce is easier with stock ownership. You can pick up the phone and "sell." Profits or earnings, and sometimes increasing dividends, are the rewards in stocks. As earnings improve, and if market conditions warrant, the price of the shares should increase.

A corporation "floats" (issues) stock in order to raise capital without paying interest or promising to give it back. In other words, you the investor help "bankroll" the company's growth. If you own growth stock, you are an entrepreneurial woman, but without the power or problems of management. A decision to buy growth stocks means you will forgo the known, fixed income of bonds or savings for the chance of sharing in a greater rate of return. You are a woman at risk!

Bonds may seem complicated to understand, but the stock market is more mysterious. The Market, as it is known, has developed a personality all its own, and we hear all kinds of reasons why "it" is doing whatever "it" is doing. For instance, the Market is down "because of profit-taking" or there was "a technical correction"; or up because of "short coverage" or so-and-so's speech "sent the Market into a slide." I especially like the phrase, "The Market thinks. . . ." Really?

But investors don't buy the Market. They buy stocks. The basic reason to buy or sell has to do with the prognosis for earnings. Many measurements exist to make predictions, such as the price of the stock in proportion to its earnings or charts that track its past value.

HOW TO BUY OR SELL A STOCK

There is nothing magical or mysterious about placing an order for a stock with a broker. Assuming you have done your homework, your conversation can be very simple. Here's how.

Open an account with the firm of your choosing. This can be initiated on the telephone, and you will be required to sign certain paperwork to open the account. They will need to know your name, address, phone, Social Security number, and other general financial information that verifies your trading qualifications in line with regulations. Also, most firms will require a certain amount of cash in a newly opened account before you purchase, or delivery of the security you will sell, prior to taking an order. This is not usually true once you have established a business relationship with them.

If you wish to buy or sell a stock, tell your broker, "I want to buy (or sell) some Megabucks Corp. common stock. What was the last trade?"

The broker will be able to tell you immediately the price at which the stock most recently sold, the bid and the ask, unless it is a less-known or less-traded issue. Most stocks that are frequently traded appear on the broker's screen as accessed by the stock symbol (which is not the abbreviation that appears in the newspaper). Assuming the value is close to what you expect from your information, you may place the order. Otherwise, find out first why the difference. Maybe trading has "stopped" because of sudden volume demand to buy or sell and orders cannot be matched.

"Buy 100 shares of Megabucks Corp. common at the market" means you will take whatever price is asked when your order hits the floor. In this computer age, that is very fast.

Or you can specify a limit price. You will only buy at a

price you designate: "Buy 100 shares of Megabucks Corp. common at 34½ [or better is implied]."

You may also state if this limit order is for the "day only" or "good until canceled." It is your contractual responsibility in the latter case to cancel. You don't want a surprise trade months later.

Limit orders can be a good idea with stocks with a large spread between bid and ask, such as some "over-the-counter" trades. There are other variations, but the idea is that you set the terms by which the stock is bought or sold.

The same system works for both buys and sells. That's all it takes. This is your oral contract with the broker to buy or sell, and as with all contracts it is binding. The written confirmation you receive in the mail is just an after-the-fact written record. You don't get to change your mind.

Finally, on a "buy," you must say how you want the stock registered; on a "sell," you must inform the broker of how the stock is registered. It can be "held in street name," which means the firm holds it for you in its name, but designated within your own account, or it can be registered directly to your name (or jointly). You may take "delivery" of the actual certificate, or, if you have the brokerage firm keep it, you may still choose which registration you wish, in your name "in safe-keeping" or in street name. Many investors prefer to keep securities at the brokerage firm for easy trading and for convenience of paperwork. It takes care of dividends, splits, and other activity. You receive notice of all activity on statements, including an end-of-the-year summary that is convenient for tax purposes. There is federal insurance for securities as with some bank accounts, although money market funds are usually excluded from the insurance protection. The amount of insurance varies. Ask the firm about it if you have a large account.

If you buy stock on margin you have borrowed money from the firm. In that case, you must leave the stock certificate with them in street name as collateral.

Since inactive accounts may be charged holding fees, if you don't plan to trade you may wish to take delivery of the certificate and put it in your safe deposit box. Warning: Lost securities will put you to a great deal of trouble, so don't lose them! It is a good idea to keep a photocopy at home for easy reference.

As part of the buy or sell contract, you must pay for or deliver the stock within five business days (Saturdays, Sundays, and holidays don't count). The confirmation will show "net price," which includes commissions and fees. This record should match the oral trade and should match the monthly statement. Always check it for quantity, price, and security name. It is a truism on Wall Street that errors tend to get more costly as time goes by. Keep your records *accurate and up-to-date.*

If you sell a stock and you have the certificate, you will need to sign it, usually on the bottom line, to make it negotiable. You should also write in the name of the brokerage firm on the blank that says "the power of attorney" so that no one else can cash it in. "Stock power" is a separate signature form that serves the same purpose.

TIPS FOR SMART INVESTMENT RECORD KEEPING

PROFIT AND LOSS RECORDS

In addition to confirmation slips and monthly statements of the activity in your account, it is always wise to keep your own records in a financial notebook. For example, for the purchase of a stock, note the name, quantity, price, and date of purchase. When you sell the stock, also note the price and date of sale. To calculate your net profit (or loss) on the transaction, add commissions and other fees to the purchase price and subtract that amount from the sale price. Total purchase cost and total sale price are all you need to calculate your profit or loss for tax purposes.

NAME	AMT	PUR DATE	@PRICE PER SHR	TOT PUR COST	SALE DATE	@PRICE PER SHR	TOT SALE PRICE	PROFIT (LOSS)
XYZ	100	3/4/86	@$15	$1,535	4/2/87	@17	$1,650	$115

DIVIDENDS

Note the date, ratio of splits, and amount of dividend increases (or decreases) on any stock you hold.

STOCK TOTAL RETURN

Also note any dividend paid to you while you hold the stock. Your total return on a stock is the dividend and the profit (or loss) from its sale. In our example, XYZ paid an annual dividend of $1 per share. You purchased 100 shares, held them for a year, so you will have received $100 in dividends. This figure added to your profit of $115 from sale of the stock ($100 plus $115 equals $215) is your total return. Divide your total return by your total purchase cost to find the yield on your investment ($215 divided by $1,535 equals 14 percent). Not a bad investment, but remember that you are taxed on both dividends and profit. (And remember, too, that dividends are taxed as you earn them, while profit and loss are tax-deferred until the time you sell.) Your net yield must take into account the cost of taxes, calculated on the basis of your own tax bracket.

DIVIDEND YIELD

You cannot predict whether your stock will go up or down, and therefore increase or decrease your overall yield from the investment. You can, however, predict your dividend yield at the time of purchase or before you purchase. When asking the price of a stock, you can also ask for the yield based on its dividend. To calculate it yourself, divide the dividend per share by the stock price per share. Again in our example, XYZ pays an annual dividend of $1 per share, and the purchase price was $15 per share: $1 divided by $15 equals 6.7 percent. Of course, the higher the price of the stock, the lower your yield as long as the dividend hasn't changed. This figure is useful to enable you to compare the expected yield on this investment with other investments. If the dividend increases, so will your yield. Remember to always calculate your yield on the basis of your purchase price. The newspaper yields are based on the current price of the stock.

BOND RECORDS OR BANK CDs

You should also keep similarly complete and up-to-date records of your investment in bonds or bank CDs. In particular, note the yield of the bond at the time of purchase (which is often different from the stated coupon rate).

PURCHASE DATE	FACE AMOUNT	NAME	COST PER UNIT	TOTAL COST	YIELD TO MATURITY
9/10/83	10,000	QRS Municipal Bond, Series C 4¾ %	84.191	$8,419.10	8%
		due 1/1/90			

Also note special conditions, such as when a bond is "callable," the date the issuer can pay you before maturity. Under these conditions, your principal is returned to you and no further interest is paid. Some call features require the issuer to pay a prepayment penalty to compensate you for loss of interest and possibly lower yield on your next investment.

REAL ESTATE RECORDS

Real estate records are more complicated. Keep a separate page for each piece of property you own, noting what you paid for it, known as the "cost basis," plus improvements to the property, date, and amount. When the time comes to sell the property, improvements that raise your cost basis in the property will lower your tax liability. Keep records of all your closing costs for both the purchase and the sale of the property and receipts for all improvements. And certainly keep all the official records.

Keeping careful up-to-date records will help you gain self-confidence and respect from the financial professionals with whom you are dealing. And although it might seem complicated .at first, it becomes much easier with experience. If you're not sure at first what records to keep, don't be afraid to ask.

ASSUMING GREATER RISK

All stock purchases involve some risk. But to increase the possibility of greater reward, many investors take on greater risk. The investments in the upper part of the investment triangle exhibit this characteristic. Women often find the complicated rules of these investment games, which are usually played with leverage, forbidding. Leverage means borrowing *someone else's money* to increase the funds available for investment and thus, it is hoped, achieve a greater rate of return. The mortgage on your house or condo is a form of leverage. So is buying stocks on "margin." In both, you can lose your investment if you can't repay the loan. Naturally, the greater the leverage the greater the risk.

HOW LEVERAGE WORKS

Leverage magnifies profit or loss and is a characteristic of higher-risk investments, like commodity trading, which is at the risky pinnacle of the investment triangle. For example, if the future contract (the unit for sale) of 38,000 pounds of pork bellies (bacon) has a value of $22,000, the margin requirement might be $2,000, or about 10 percent of the total commodity value. (Brokerage firms periodically determine the margin based on their assignment of market risk.) Unlike stock margin, this requirement is considered "good faith" money. It is not a loan and no interest is charged because you have not yet completed the purchase (or sale) of the commodity. But you have contracted to buy (or sell) the pork bellies at $22,000 and will make payment (or deliver the commodity) on a specified future date. You may close out this contractual right at any time to take a profit or loss. For example, if you purchased pork bellies at $22,000 and the market value of this contract increases to $24,000, your profit would be $2,000 beyond the original $2,000 you put up as margin requirement. That represents a 100 percent profit on your money, and illustrates the lure of leverage to speculators in commodity trading. On the other hand, if the contract decreases in value by $2,000, you would be wiped out by 100 percent. And if there is any further decrease in value, you would be forced to repay those losses, too—within twenty-four hours. In that case, you'd probably never eat bacon again. Because of unlimited potential loss, brokerage firms ascertain ahead of time if you can afford to play the commodity game.

The leverage we are more familiar with is in real estate. And under the old tax laws, it was often to your advantage to invest in real estate with little or no money as a down payment and some form of mortgage to cover the rest. The new tax laws have changed that picture, but now as then, whatever the investment: The greater the leverage, the greater the risk.

A Number 2 Wife in her thirties, mother of one child, came to one of my educational investment seminars and then made an appointment to see me. She was concerned with her new husband's asset management plans. In her own name, she owned the modest house in which they lived, that had a reasonable mortgage, and a bank account of about $25,000. He was encouraging her to borrow some of the equity in her house for another real estate investment.

He owned $10,000 in stock, which he earmarked for the education of his three children. He also owned a large portfolio of real estate with a market value estimated at approximately $500,000 but which had mortgages of $350,000. Not all of the property broke even on an after-tax basis. He reasoned that inflation, increased property values, and the leverage would make him rich. She was worried.

The lack of diversification of their assets (85 percent was in real estate) was a potential problem. The real estate might not increase in value, and changes in the tax law could eliminate some of the deductions. They had insufficient liquidity for other emergencies. It also turned out that he had very little life insurance despite his debts and obligations to his children. More important, if their dual income were jeopardized, say if either lost a job, they would be in real trouble.

Unfortunately, this was not a "joint-decision" marriage when it came to finance. She was afraid to tell her husband that she had been to see me, and was unable to convince him of her wishes to diversify, to use less leverage, to be more conservative. As a "businessman," the way he characterized himself, he relied only on his own financial opinions. The marriage did not change this. The last I heard, she resisted his appeal for further leveraging of her home. I wonder if the tax law changes affected his portfolio strategy.

You can get leverage without borrowing. When you buy a stock option—allowing you the right to buy a stock at a certain price for a specified period of time—you have leverage. You only put up a small sum of money for the option, say a few hundred dollars, but you have potential ownership control of the stock itself. Since it is a substitute for the stock, if the stock goes up, as you speculated, your option becomes more valuable and you can take a profit. If not, you may lose all your money.

Some options are used as risk protection, or "hedges." They may guarantee you the right to sell your stock at a certain price ("put" it to someone else), or grant you some of the paper profit in an immediate cash "premium." In return, you must be willing to give up the stock or have it "called" away from you. Options come in two varieties: puts and calls.

To "up the ante" even more, you can get leverage on leverage: options on commodities.

OTHER SPECULATIVE INVESTMENTS

Other financial games include *index options,* which provide a way to buy or sell broad market indexes. There are a variety of them that permit you to guess "up" or "down," and "when" (much more difficult) for the Dow Jones, the New York Stock Exchange, the Technology Index, and many more indexes.

Another way to speculate is by selling that which you don't own: *shorting.* If you put up margin money, you can do this. You are "borrowing" stock for the sale from the brokerage firm. The idea is that you expect what you sold to go down, so you can buy it back cheaper and keep the difference. In contrast to the optimistic "bull," you are a pessimist or "bear." Now this game—selling what you don't have—sounds like a strange idea, a boys' street game. Yet think about it, "down" is just as fair a way to make money as "up"—provided you are right. Wrong assumptions, of course, cost money. If the stock goes up, you will owe more money since eventually you must "cover" your purchase and "buy in" the stock you sold.

I have left precious metals and collectibles for last

because their place in the investment triangle is so contro-versial.

If you love gold and think it is the only "real thing" out there, you might consider it a conservative investment—absolutely necessary for your peace of mind. Safe deposit boxes here and abroad, as well as some backyard hiding places, are full of it. If, however, you put most of your assets in gold when it reached $800 per ounce, and it now sells in the $400s, you might consider it a high-risk investment.

Gold has been very volatile in the last decade, and profits have been mostly for short-term traders. In addition, gold has become political since the boycott of South African Krugerrands, adding to its riskiness as an investment. Gold, like money, means more to people than its exchange value.

Even so, some women who trust gold, but not paper or coins or other metals, gladly cite historical evidence of gold as the "real thing." In particular, they are upset with devaluations of money from government printing presses and inflation. Some of these investors have had experiences in wars abroad or in the Great Depression of the 1930s.

Goldie loves gold. She keeps it in her safe deposit box and at home, along with silver, diamonds, and foreign currencies—"in case of emergency." She also has plenty of cash on hand during weekends, "Just in case they close the banks." Goldie usually wears a great deal of jewelry, probably for the same reason.

I don't mean to make fun of these fears. After all, she may be right! All of Goldie's favorite investments are what are called "hard assets"—things with an intrinsic value not dependent on earnings, profits, or business acumen. Their value is determined largely by supply and demand. I have observed that people who like gold often like all hard assets, which they say constitute a "store of value." Real estate and natural resources are in this category. Hard assets are very different from liquid assets, such as cash in hand and income flow, which are preferred by people who like to have the money coming in. Goldie had sufficient income from pensions and some rents to invest this way.

Probably every investment you can think of fits somewhere into the investment triangle. "Packaged goods" for group buying, such as mutual funds, limited partnerships, and unit trusts, are variations on a theme. Whatever is their investment *content and objective* will tell you where it fits in the triangle. Now the important question is: Where do *you* fit in the investment triangle?

10

Catch a Falling Star and Put It in Your Pocket

INVESTMENT STRATEGIES

THE ideal investment would have no risk. It would have a high rate of growth and produce good income. It would be easily marketable, or "liquid." And, of course, it would be tax-resistant and inflation-proof. Just what you had in mind! In the real world, alas, you usually have to choose among the benefits and risks of what's available, whether careers, men, or investments. *There is no perfect investment for all needs for all times!*

The best way to consider investments is by their objectives—what they will do for you. After all, you invest to achieve a financial goal, not just to read it on your statement or because a broker has told you what "a good deal" it is. But there are a few general rules that apply whatever your financial goal:

Understand what you buy. For example, really read the prospectus to find the objective of the investment, how the objective is to be achieved, the cost, the track record, management expertise, and the investment's projected time frame. Don't buy options if you don't understand them just because your investment adviser does.

Diversify your investments. Who needs all their assets in a house sitting on the San Andreas fault?

Compare your prospective investment with other investment opportunities. But don't do it without logic. If you want the liquidity of a money market fund, don't compare it with a twenty-year, tax-free bond. Compare apples with apples, not with oranges or yogurt.

Consider supply and demand. That is what making money is really about. Timing is also a key element in buying and selling investments. Information and instinct don't hurt, either. Just when to buy and sell, and whether to make a profit or take a loss, are hard decisions to make.

Let reasons rule. Risks can be calculated to some degree. "Buying panics" are the wrong time. Perceiving what might be needed next is more in line with that wonderful down-to-earth common sense women have attained from running their households and their lives.

And yes, the bottom line is *do what is right for you.* Your personal investment triangle should be suited to *your* needs and wishes. If you are applying the lessons in this book, your financial plan is well on its way.

MAKING INVESTMENT DECISIONS

By now you know that investing is really a type of comparison shopping. When I shop for an investment, I have learned never to begin without considering seven Reality Pointers, and my common sense, as decision-making aids. They incorporate all that has gone before in this book—

only now is the time to apply them to a "real world" decision.

At a recent social function I met Ms. Innocent Impatience, a fifty-five-year-old widow. A novice in the investment world, Ms. Impatience has been educating herself by paying for a series of seminars on real estate. She is extremely eager to purchase real property for investment purposes. She is sure that if she learns the "secrets" of investment success, she can become rich the way others have. She figures that she just needs the knowledge, and as she speaks, I recall all the TV advertising I have seen about real estate seminars.

Innocent tells me that the most important thing she has learned is to find a piece of real estate with the right financing. "Right financing," according to her teacher, means a low, assumable mortgage or, better yet, no money down at all. She asks if I think it is a good idea for her to buy some real estate, considering her circumstances. She is satisfied with living in a rental house in an area where real estate values have been increasing rapidly. She has a small amount of capital, under $50,000, presently in a money market fund at a brokerage firm. She is concerned that interest rates are falling. Retirement from compulsory work is her main goal, and this money is insufficient for that purpose. The income from her public library job is modest.

The questions Innocent asked me are common ones. But there are other, more fundamental questions she, or any potential investor, needs to ask, and answer, before making investment decisions. They include the meaning of "investing," the elements of decision-making, and the difference between an estimation (which is really an informed opinion based on reasonable assumptions) and guesses or "long shots" (which are for speculators and gamblers). It is this information that you, I, and Innocent should put in our pockets when going shopping for investments. Falling stars, though more romantic, are far less dependable!

POINTER #1: REVIEW YOUR PERSONAL FINANCIAL GOALS

Investing without having set down your personal financial goals is like shopping without a list. You are vulnerable to impulse buying that may not suit your needs when you get them home. Each time you plan to invest, review the goals you have written in your notebook.

Let's apply this pointer to the case of Innocent Impatience. Innocent's circumstances and goal tell me that she is near retirement age (pension plans typically begin paying out at between ages fifty-nine and sixty-five), so she really cannot afford much risk to her limited savings. In case of losses, she could not make them up again in her later years. She has little diversification for safety. In the next five years, it would be desirable for her to own a residence, preferably one with some available rental space, which could provide additional income—especially income that can be adjusted for inflation. This would fix her major cost of living, her housing, which could be particularly important if she is on a modest, fixed pension income and inflation heats up.

POINTER #2: KNOW THE FACTS

Ask the right questions and really listen to the answers. If you are purchasing real estate, as in Innocent's case (or other equity investments, such as stock), ask these questions:

• *Why* make this investment at this time? What is the basis for assuming that you can make money?

• What is the projected *period of time* you will hold the investment?

• What are the numbers? How much *appreciation* as a percentage of your capital can you reasonably project? How much *cash flow,* if any, can you reasonably expect? For your tax bracket, how much *in tax savings dollars,* if any, can you reasonably expect? Not all tax benefits have disappeared under the new tax laws, although they are considerably less because tax brackets are lower. Use whatever is available to calculate the pluses of this investment.

• What is the *"worst case"* scenario, as well as a more reasonable loss possibility? Can you afford such a loss?

• Can you control the *risk?*

• If you decide to terminate the investment early, what can you expect in the way of *penalties,* either implied or designated?

• If not your sole ownership, *who controls* or *manages* the investment? What will they get out of it, such as fees and financial benefits? Do they have a conflict of interest with you? Are they qualified for the job? And, of course, are they honest?

• What are the *costs and commitments* while buying and selling the investment?

If Innocent decides to find an interim investment while looking for real estate, and chooses an interest-bearing vehicle, she would need to ask the following questions:

• What is the *rate of interest?* That is, what is the *current yield* on the cash ("cash on cash") you are putting up? And what is the *yield to maturity* (on bonds) that would account for more money you might receive on maturity?

• When is your *principal returned,* or when does the loan *mature?*

• What is the *quality* or *rating* of the borrower? What is the rating scale, and what do each of the ratings mean?

• How *liquid is the resale market* if you decide to sell prior to maturity? How might you expect to come out?

• What is the *"worst case"* scenario that might be possible?

• Are there any *commissions* or *fees* beyond those about which you have been told?

You know how to shop for personal and household goods. You understand what you are getting into and the questions to ask. Investments are no different. No honorable sellers of investments will object to your asking valid, intelligent questions. They will recognize it as a mark of good business. You will be respected more, and probably be given better service.

Generally, as the buyer of any investment, you should be aware of what the seller gets out of the deal as well as what benefits are yours. Then you will understand if it is fair to you.

Since Innocent's primary purpose is to shop for real estate, here are some facts that she should keep in mind. First, real estate is an equity investment. There are no guaranteed returns. Although real estate value has traditionally moved with inflation, it may not always do so. Tax policy and higher brackets had something to do with the price increases as more investors desiring tax protection chased available property. And since the inflation rate is lower today than in the recent past, the reasons to buy should be carefully reconsidered.

In past eras, the major reason to buy real estate was cash flow—or cash flow potential (increasing rents). Appreciation occurred because of greater cash flow—giving more value to the property—and that takes time, and loss of liquidity.

Real estate investments in Innocent's region do not appear to offer good cash flow, if any. Furthermore, Innocent does not have much liquidity, which is a dangerous situation for her to be in if the property has to be held with negative cash flow, or even no cash flow, for a prolonged period of time. Just the real estate commission of 6 percent will take some appreciation to break even.

Innocent's investment strategy, in my opinion, should be to stay relatively liquid in short-term and intermediate investments, such as money market funds, U.S. Treasury obligations, bank certificates of deposit, or high-quality corporate bonds: four to seven years should be the maximum length of the investments. At the time of this recommendation, interest rates were very uncertain, and for further protection I recommended varying maturities within that time frame. This would keep her in a liquid position and give her some cash flow to build her asset base. And it would also give her some time to look around for an investment opportunity in real estate, which is still her goal.

POINTER #3: SET AN INVESTMENT GOAL AND MONITOR IT

Have an objective in mind for the investment. For example, if you think a stock could go up 40 percent in the next year, plan to consider sale at that point, unless new facts give you reason to believe the stock will go higher.

On the other side, consider risk control methods. You may decide ahead of time that if a loss of 15 to 20 percent occurs, you will sell immediately. Clients complain that their broker never tells them when to sell, but that decision, as with the purchase, is the investor's. As a broker, I have always found this to be a difficult problem. If a stock is up, the client wants to hold for more profit; if it's down, she often wants to wait to get even. We sometimes get emotionally attached to "our" stocks (brokers are not excluded from this phenomenon). The wisdom of a past decision is usually measured by how favorable the results were. We remember selectively.

Trading controls can be set with *stop orders, good until canceled.* You instruct your broker to place a stop price of your choosing, one that is below the market price. What you are saying is that if the stock should go down to that price, or below it, you want an automatic sale. This can be a good way to protect against large losses and protect profits. You may also use the technique of a "trailing stop," which means you simply raise the stop price as the stock moves up to protect profits. The possible problem in using "stops" is that if they are too close to the current market price, ordinary trading zigzags will take you out. I recommend a stop price 15 to 20 percent below market value, depending on the stock's volatility.

A woman invests $20,000 in a speculation of her choosing—a high-risk medical research stock. This is money that she says she can afford to lose if she is wrong. The stock doubles. I call her and tell her the price, and ask her what she wants to do. I do not make her decision, but she decides to take the profit. Subsequently, the stock moves up significantly. She phones me, furious, claiming that it is my fault she sold, and she has "lost money because I phoned her." She says that if I hadn't called her she wouldn't have sold at that time. I didn't hear from her again, but I noticed that within a year the stock had dropped way below her original purchase price. Speculations have a way of doing that!

Monitoring your investments to see if they are performing as expected is a way to control risk. Changing your mind is okay. Change is part of the mechanism of the investment world.

POINTER #4: COMPARE

You don't have to buy the first pair of shoes you try on. And neither do you have to invest your money in the same way all the time, or take whatever is offered to you. There are a variety of ways in which to invest your money. So you should compare your proposed investment two ways: first, with others of the same type, and second, with others at different risk levels. It is particularly helpful to compare an investment geared to long-term growth with a low-risk, passive investment. This will show you whether the expected results are worth the risk and the commitment of your money for a longer time.

Assuming you have done your homework and know the facts and goal of the proposed investment, some very simple mental math can give you the needed comparison. Here is an example.

Hypothetically, a real estate investment for a seven- to ten-year holding period has a present positive cash flow of a certain amount per year after subtracting mortgage payments, insurance, taxes, repairs, and maintenance from the rental income. Because of estimated rent increases in the neighborhood, you can expect that the cash flow will increase at some yearly average rate over the life of the investment.

Now look at any tax benefits: depreciation or interest deductions that apply to your tax bracket. Operating expenses will also affect the bottom line. Don't forget to include as an expense the value of the lost income from your downpayment. If you put money into the property, it is no longer earning market rates of interest in an alternative investment.

Perhaps, with the help of a good real estate agent, you can make a reasonable estimation of the appreciation potential. You must assume some number before entering into such a deal. On the page opposite is a hypothetical example of a rough calculation.

Your investment just about breaks even—not counting the real estate commission if you sell and if your appreciation number is right. A greater average appreciation rate— over the holding period projected—would be necessary for significant profit.

Property cost	$150,000
Money down	50,000
Tax bracket assumed	28%

Outgo:

Interest on mortgage @11%	$ 11,000
Taxes and insurance	2,000
Operating expenses and repairs	4,000
Loss of interest on down payment (assumes 7%)	3,500
Total	$ 20,500

Income:

Rent	$ 10,200
Tax savings: depreciation, interest deduction, operating expenses, and repairs	4,900
Appreciation: 4% annually	6,000
Total	$ 21,100

From these calculations, you have an estimated income and appreciation number to compare against similar investments in real estate or low-risk, fixed-income securities.

Once you have made these comparisons, the next question is: Is it worth it?

Seasoned investors make these comparisons as a matter of course. They know the relationship among these kinds of numbers most of the time. Don't forget to use the Rule 72 as described in Chapter 7 for compound interest or estimated inflation effects.

POINTER #5: THE PAST IS NOT A TRACK RECORD OF THE FUTURE

It is important to know how an investment has performed in the past. It is equally important to know about the record of its promoters and owners—their reliability, honesty, and success. This is part of your collection of factual information, which you will be sure to read in a prospectus or descriptive literature. This past record, however, is just that: the past.

You can assume the same results for the future only if all circumstances and conditions remain the same, and that, of course, is impossible. People often learn the wrong lessons from past performance and are overwhelmed by them. For example, one cannot predict the future rate of inflation by past charts: indications are not the same as predictions.

Past inflation caused many conservative investors to lose money in high-quality, long-term bonds, while real estate owners and speculators made lots of money. But is the lesson to be drawn from this that orphans and widows should now all be in real estate?

POINTER #6: ALL INVESTMENTS ARE SUBJECT TO BASIC ECONOMICS: SUPPLY AND DEMAND

This is the most commonsensical pointer of them all, and the key to making good estimations. If you understand this concept, you are way ahead of most investors.

If you buy what others do not want very much, it will be cheap. You may sell it for more dollars when more people want it—unless you bought stock in a girdle company (remember them?) when pantyhose were being introduced to the world. Sometimes you might buy it when people are just beginning to want it, and still make a profit. Once everybody wants it, think red flag. Remember the game of pass the hot potato?

Making money can simply be the correct perception of supply and demand. And some women have a natural talent for this, just as some always wear the right clothes for every occasion.

POINTER #7: INVESTMENTS RUN IN CYCLES

Times change. Economics change. Supply and demand change. Tax laws change.

The perception of "timeliness" for an investment is a key to success. Know the economic climate in which you are investing by reading, listening, watching, and interpreting current events. No one can do more than that. Many events are discounted way ahead of an actual happening because investors are reading "into" the news ahead of time. Different investments behave in different ways under different economic conditions. As we discussed earlier, growth-oriented investments are not as successful during recessions. Fixed-income investments do not do well during increasing inflation.

Uncertainty is the circumstance most disliked by serious investors. Speculators, on the other hand, love uncertainty because they can win or lose high stakes. During uncertain times, between cycles, you might choose to do nothing. In this case, "nothing" means staying very liquid in cash substitutes. You do not always have to be invested (contrary to what your investment broker may tell you). If it is late in the game for the investment of your choice, wait until a more propitious time and, maybe, a different investment. If you are uncertain as to which way the economy is going, wait until there is "more writing on the wall."

YOUR INVESTMENT PLAN

Your own investment plan, finding the star to put in your pocket, must suit your personal needs and risk level. Whatever you are considering buying, apply the seven Reality Pointers. If it passes this test, you can be assured that you are making an informed choice.

11

Put Yourself in the Picture

TYPICAL FINANCIAL PLANS

EVERY woman is unique. We are all different in our ages and temperaments, our financial situations, and our needs and goals. But there are, I think, two things we all should have in common. The first is the need to understand our financial picture and the financial opportunities that are available to us. The second is the need to devise a comprehensive and realistic financial plan to take advantage of those opportunities.

I hope I have, in the preceding chapters, given you the information necessary to assess your own financial picture. You should now know what you own and what you owe, your income, your outgo, and what you can save and invest to achieve your financial goals. Armed with that knowledge, now is the time to put it all together in a financial plan. Obviously, no single financial plan is right for every woman. But in the pages that follow I present a broad spectrum of plans offering different strategies organized by each woman's circumstances and by her investment preference.

These plans are not constructed to represent real women. They are meant to be typical of women in different stages of life, having different sources of income and assets, and in different family situations. You may find one among them that approximates your own unique situation. If not, you can use the format of these plans and fill in your own details.

Think of it this way. You are about to start on a trip. You know where you are and where you want to go. What is the first thing you tuck into your handbag or glove compartment? A road map. And that is what your financial plan is: a road map that will tell you how to achieve your life goals. Write it down. Refer to it as you begin your journey and as you proceed along the way. Review and modify it as circumstances change. Remember: Both your own finances and the economic environment are subject to continuous and sometimes dramatic change. But whatever your circumstances, whatever your destination, one thing is certain: You'll never get anywhere unless you put your financial plan into action. Even the most detailed road map is useless unless you take the trip.

FINANCIAL PLAN #1

DESCRIPTION (who she is)

AGE:	in her 20s
FAMILY STATUS:	single, no children
CAREER:	government employee, opportunity for advancement
PERSONALITY PROFILE:	risk orientation: middle range
	self-perception and expectations: educated, middle-class life-style, marriage

FINANCIAL SITUATION (where she is)

NET WORTH:	(gift from grandmother)	$20,000
ANNUAL INCOME:	Salary	$26,500
	Investments	600
	Total	$27,100

FINANCIAL PLAN #1 (Continued)

ANNUAL EXPENSES:	Fixed	$22,000	80%
	Discretionary	5,100	20%
	Total	$27,100	100%
PORTFOLIO DIVERSIFICATION:	Income assets (short-term)	$20,000	100%
	Growth assets		0
	Hard assets		0
	Speculative assets		0
	Total	$20,000	100%
DEBT:	(auto, credit cards, college)	$11,000	
RATIO DEBT TO ASSETS:	($11,000 divided by $20,000)		55%
ANNUAL SAVING AMOUNT:			0

OTHER FUTURE INCOME: retirement plan if she stays, inheritance not known at this time.

FINANCIAL GOALS (where she wants to be)

to invest her lump-sum gift wisely; others: to have a higher standard of living, make more money in her career

INVESTMENT STRATEGY (how to do it)

This young woman feels "rich" with her newly acquired investment assets. But using some of this money to decrease her debts should be first on her list, before thoughts of investing or buying the "better things of life." And she should begin a serious savings effort to increase her asset base for future security. Her present cost of living can be modified to allow for monthly savings. She could aim at a minimum of $100 a month. Income from her job should rise annually, and some portion of the increase should be earmarked for savings and investment.

In particular, the auto and credit card debt, at high rates of interest, should be eliminated—$5,000 of her savings (earning a much lower rate of interest) would take care of these. The school loan at a more reasonable rate of interest and with a generous time allowance can be paid off monthly as scheduled.

Her goal of a higher standard of living is unrealistic at this time. She should sacrifice a little now for more financial independence later on. By focusing on saving for a specific purpose she can discipline herself. For example, she appreciates saving for the possibility of full-time graduate school to increase her earning potential, or if her job advancement is satisfactory, saving for the purchase of a condo as her residence.

She recognizes that she has too much money in a short-term savings account to achieve any significant asset growth. After paying off the high-interest debts, it is advisable for her to invest about 50 percent in mutual funds of high-quality growth stocks, since the stock market is currently advancing rapidly, and reinvesting dividends and capital gains as long as market conditions warrant. She will still have sufficient emergency money easily available. And she agrees to a regular savings plan as a worthwhile trade-off for her objectives.

FINANCIAL PLAN #2

DESCRIPTION (who she and her husband are)

AGE:	in their 30s
FAMILY STATUS:	married, no children
CAREER:	she is an MBA graduate, junior executive, her husband is a lawyer
PERSONALITY PROFILE:	risk orientation: high-risk self-perception and expectations: great optimism, to be rich

FINANCIAL SITUATION (where they are)

NET WORTH:	(family gifts and savings)	$125,000	
ANNUAL INCOME:	Combined salaries	$ 92,300	
	Investments	1,100	
	Total	$ 93,400	
ANNUAL EXPENSES:	Fixed	$ 50,400	54%
	Discretionary	$ 43,000	46%
	Total	$ 93,400	100%

FINANCIAL PLAN #2 (Continued)

PORTFOLIO
DIVERSIFICATION:

Income assets (short-term)	$ 12,500	10%
Growth assets, stocks	75,000	60%
Hard assets	0	
Speculative assets, options	37,500	30%
Total	$125,000	100%

DEBT: (school loans)　　　　　　　　　　$ 17,500

RATIO OF DEBTS TO ASSETS: ($17,500 divided by $125,000)　　14%

ANNUAL SAVING AMOUNT:　　　　　　　　$ 10,000

OTHER FUTURE INCOME: Inheritance uncertain—both sets of parents are still young and in middle-income range

FINANCIAL GOALS (where they want to be)

to buy a house
others: husband wants to set up his own law practice, to have children

INVESTMENT STRATEGY (how to do it)

This couple needs to save more money on a monthly basis to get a capital base for the life-style they envision. Houses are expensive; a law practice will require funds for set-up and operation costs during a client-building period. Parenting entails other expenses: either one of them must stay at home during the early years (resulting in less income), or they will have to pay for professional baby care. And there are many other expenses associated with having and caring for a child, including life insurance on one or both wage-earners. Their list of "wants" requires them to reduce living expenses now and save for the future.

While saving more, they do not need to invest most of their money in conservative income-oriented investments. With two high-level incomes, they can afford more risk and they believe in growth stocks. They keep timely records on the performance of their mutual funds and note the financial news, alert to potential economic changes.

Financial planning alerts them to their real priority: the

establishing of the husband's law practice. This is in line with their feelings about taking risk for what they perceive is a potentially significant reward. They will need the money invested in mutual funds to take on a venture of investing in his career. The wife is at some risk here, since her funds are also being pledged to this purpose. Both are businesspeople and find a practical resolution of the issue in a written contract between them for her fair compensation should the marriage not last.

Also, they decide to reconsider their speculations in options. As inexperienced option buyers, they have discovered the difficulty in "winning" consistently in the option markets. They compromise by buying a professionally managed option fund, which takes on various strategies dependent on market conditions as perceived by the managers of the fund. This investment will be more aggressive than their other mutual funds, but restricted to their original investment amount, which is all they are willing to lose.

The house goal will wait until both careers are on track. The timing on when to have children is not yet resolved.

FINANCIAL PLAN #3

DESCRIPTION (who she is)

AGE:	in her 30s
FAMILY STATUS:	divorced: 1 child, age 9
CAREER:	administrative assistant
PERSONALITY PROFILE:	risk orientation: middle range self-perception and expectations: successful career-woman struggling to maintain self and child in appropriate style, hopes to remarry

FINANCIAL SITUATION (where she is)

NET WORTH:	(divorce settlement)	$ 8,600
ANNUAL INCOME:	Salary	$23,900
	Child support (not dependable)	4,800
	Investments	600
	Total	$29,300

FINANCIAL PLAN #3 (Continued)

ANNUAL EXPENSES:	Fixed	$28,700	99%
	Discretionary	1,700	1%
	Total	$30,400	100%

PORTFOLIO DIVERSIFICATION:			
	Income assets (short-term, credit union account)	$ 8,800	56%
	Growth assets (stock mutual fund)	6,800	44%
	Hard assets	0	
	Speculative assets	0	
	Term life insurance through employment	$10,000	
	Total	$15,600	100%

DEBT:	(auto)	7,000	
RATIO OF DEBT TO ASSETS: ($7,000 divided by $15,600)			45%
ANNUAL SAVING AMOUNT:			0
OTHER FUTURE INCOME: possible small inheritance, but not soon			

FINANCIAL GOALS (where she wants to be)

> to make it month to month
> others: child's education, her own future security

INVESTMENT STRATEGY (how to do it)

First, this woman urgently needs to budget her income. She is not making it month-to-month. In round numbers, her expenses look like this:

FIXED EXPENSES		Annual
Federal income tax		$ 2,300
State income tax		500
FICA		1,600
State disability insurance		300
Medical and dental insurance (company pays all)		0
Housing		
rent	@$825/mo	9,900
insurance		200

Food
    at home   2,100
    lunches: self   600
            child   300
Utilities
    water   0
    electricity   1,000
    telephone   500
Childcare (after school and sitters)   2,000
Auto
    insurance   700
    loan + principal   2,900
    repairs and maintenance   500
    gas   800
Clothing
    self   1,200
    child   300
Credit card interest   300
Hair dresser   400
Child's haircuts   100
Pharmaceuticals and personal care products   200
    Total $28,700

DISCRETIONARY EXPENSES
Entertainment   500
Products for the home   100
Association memberships and subscriptions   100
Allowances and miscellaneous expenses for child   200
Gifts, including Christmas   500
Vacation and travel   300
    Total $ 1,700

This woman's total annual expenses, fixed and discretionary, are $30,400. Her total annual income is $29,300. She is living beyond her means. Her fixed expenses take most of her income, and when the father does not help, she uses her savings. There are no funds for an unexpected emergency.

1. She must cut back on her expenses. The first area to consider is the most expensive one: her housing cost. If she finds an apartment for $750 a month, she would save $900 a year. She cannot reduce taxes, disability, FICA, so she must spend less on all her discretionary purchases and fixed ones where possible.

2. She decides to use the mutual fund investment to pay off the auto and credit cards, both of which have high interest charges. The mutual fund is not appropriate for her present circumstances because she cannot afford any risk and needs to address her cash flow problem. By eliminating financing of her auto and credit cards, she saves an annual amount of $3,200 and still maintains $8,600 in savings for emergencies. With less costly housing, she saves a total of $4,100. This works better.

3. She decides to take advantage of an employee benefit, $200,000 of group life insurance for the benefit of her child. At a cost of $65, it is a worthwhile protection.

4. Once her savings have reached $10,000, she has decided to restart her "growth" portfolio by utilizing what she believes is a "good deal": a company stock purchase plan funded by deductions from her paycheck. For every $1 she invests, the company invests $.75 up to 10 percent of her salary. This is the best she is able to do until her salary increases. What she can *count on* for the future may depend solely on her earning capacity and her ability to save.

FINANCIAL PLAN #4

DESCRIPTION (who she is)

AGE:	in her 40s
FAMILY STATUS:	divorced; 1 child, age 14
CAREER:	scientist, secure position
PERSONALITY PROFILE:	risk orientation: middle range
	self-perception and expectations: successful professional with high life-style and no income worries but concerned with the economy and especially the markets, little time for investment management

FINANCIAL PLAN #4 (Continued)

FINANCIAL SITUATION (where she is)

NET WORTH:	(divorce settlement, inheritance, her own earnings)	$430,000	
ANNUAL INCOME:	Salary	$ 47,000	
	Investments	6,000	
	Child support	9,600	
	Total	$ 62,600	
ANNUAL EXPENSES:	Fixed	$ 48,600	78%
	Discretionary	15,000	22%
	Total	$ 63,600	100%
PORTFOLIO DIVERSIFICATION:	Income assets (short-term)	$ 64,500	15%
	Growth assets (business partnership)	107,500	25%
	Hard assets (home equity, jewelry, gold)	228,000	53%
	Speculative assets (research lab start-up)	21,000	5%
	Pension plan managed by the company	9,000	2%
	Group life insurance $50,000 benefit		
	Total	$430,000	100%
DEBT:	(small mortgage, loan to the lab)	$120,400	

RATIO OF DEBT TO ASSETS: ($120,400 divided by 430,000)   28%
ANNUAL SAVING AMOUNT: $ 12,000
OTHER FUTURE INCOME: an inheritance expected from father, amount unknown

FINANCIAL GOALS (where she wants to be)

to educate her child at the best private schools—father's help uncertain

others: increase assets (while maintaining liquidity) to ensure future security, use investments that can withstand severe market swings, immediately remodel house

INVESTMENT STRATEGY (how to do it)

Although the home equity and "hard assets" represent a majority of her portfolio assets, they meet this woman's comfort level. She recognizes her conservative stance and offsets it with a higher risk in two business ventures. She is knowledgeable about both of them and in close touch with the laboratory operation.

Her annual savings will grow from gradual salary increases, but the laboratory testing service may turn out to be her "cash cow," a better source of income in later years.

1. She has too much money in short-term, income-producing investments. In line with her concern for market volatility, it is recommended that she purchase a high-rated bond portfolio of sequential maturities, none longer than seven years. This strategy coupled with additional monies will allow her to "average" up and down with interest rates and require little attention while at the same time allowing relative liquidity should other investment opportunities appear.

2. For inflation protection she should upgrade and add to her portfolio of growth stocks with special attention to the energy and mineral group, since she feels these have intrinsic value for the future. This selection, although involving the stock market, is in line with her present asset profile, which favors "hard assets," and is agreeable to her. She intends to hold on to these securities for a long time and not give them attention beyond her normal semiannual review.

She can afford to continue living in the style she wishes, including the remodeling of her house. However, it is recommended that she *first* put aside a portion of her income for her daughter's education. This can be invested for security in insured certificates of deposit.

She has sought the help of a financial adviser, but makes her own informed decisions. And finally, she has been advised by her attorney to set up a "living trust" with herself as trustee. The benefits of this include an alternative trustee should she ever be incapacitated; and importantly, if she dies while her daughter is a minor a trusted custodian will guard her daughter's interests.

FINANCIAL PLAN #5

DESCRIPTION (who she and her husband are)

AGE:	in their 50s
FAMILY STATUS:	married, 2 grown children, 1 grandchild
CAREER:	homemaker, husband is a successful businessman
PERSONALITY PROFILE:	risk orientation: a *conflict,* she is worried about security; he wants to be more aggressive
	self-perception and expectations: successful, upper middle-class, she feels totally dependent on her husband

FINANCIAL SITUATION (where they are)

NET WORTH:	(profit on sale of former house, and savings)	$324,800	
ANNUAL INCOME:	His salary	$ 85,000	
	Investments	9,000	
	Total	$ 94,000	
ANNUAL EXPENSES:	Fixed	$ 56,400	60%
	Discretionary	37,600	40%
	Total	$ 94,000	100%
PORTFOLIO DIVERSIFICATION:	Income assets		
(all jointly held)	(short-term)	$ 48,750	15%
	(long-term)	100,750	31%
	Growth assets	65,000	20%
	Hard assets (home equity)	81,250	25%
	Speculative assets	29,000	9%
	Total	$324,750	100%
DEBT:	(home mortgage)	$129,900	

RATIO OF DEBT TO ASSETS: ($129,900 divided by $324,750)   40%

ANNUAL SAVING AMOUNT: $ 12,000

OTHER FUTURE INCOME: pension equal to 40% of salary, Social Security, and probable inheritance $500,000

FINANCIAL GOALS (where they want to be)

retirement at same living standard
others: tax reduction, a college education fund for their grandchild, special travel each year

INVESTMENT STRATEGY (how to do it)

Their retirement income will meet their expectations for an unchanged life-style if the inheritance comes through. If unexpected events decrease their inheritance, their savings and investments will have more importance.

Taxes are not a significant problem for them within the new tax structure. Their home mortgage is deductible and the husband's pension is tax-favored.

To accommodate the possibility of a reduced inheritance in line with the husband's more aggressive risk profile, they should increase the growth percentage of their portfolio to 40 to 50 percent. His salary is satisfactory for the next ten years or so, and the future pension provides an adequate buffer along with Social Security.

To offset the increased risk of a portfolio change and the wife's economic dependence on her husband, a $100,000 life insurance policy is recommended, adding to the $50,000 group insurance at work. A policy that accumulates tax-protected savings at a fair market rate would be appropriate.

They could set up an education fund for their grandchild by gifting as much as $20,000 per year ($10,000 from each of them without incurring estate tax liability). However, their own situation is not clear yet, so it is not advisable for them to gift the maximum at this time. They could begin with an annual amount of $5,000, investing it in a secure U.S. Treasury zero-coupon bond with a ten-year maturity. A longer-term bond is not recommended, giving them opportunity to reconsider interest rates at that time.

They wish to begin their traveling now while they are young enough to enjoy it, and can allot $5,000 to $7,000 of their annual savings for this purpose.

The wife needs to take a more active role in their financial planning and decision-making. This is agreeable to her in exchange for his fair attention to her financial opinions, which will be better informed.

In line with current economic realities, the growth investment vehicles they might consider include: stocks, business opportunities, and well-located real estate. They feel the economy continues to favor growth investments. Their investment preference is to find a multiunit rental property without negative (pretax) cash flow, but for increasing income as the years go by. They could allot about 40 percent of their assets to this purpose, converting some of their income assets and speculative assets (which would especially please the wife) to make this rearrangement. Both would be comfortable with this investment strategy.

FINANCIAL PLAN #6

DESCRIPTION (who she is)

AGE:	in her late 60s
FAMILY STATUS:	widow, 1 grown child, 3 grandchildren
CAREER:	retired teacher
PERSONALITY PROFILE:	risk orientation: very conservative, security is first
	self-perception and expectations: middle-class, respectable life-style, doesn't care to be thrifty in order to leave something for her heirs

FINANCIAL SITUATION (where she is)

NET WORTH:	(inheritance, lifetime savings)	$280,000	
ANNUAL INCOME:	Pension, Social Security	$ 18,000	
	Investments	$ 10,000	
	Total	$ 28,000	
ANNUAL EXPENSES:	Fixed	$ 25,000	87%
	Discretionary	$ 3,800	13%
		$ 28,800	100%
PORTFOLIO DIVERSIFICATION:	Income assets (short-term)	$100,800	36%
	(long-term) high-yield bonds)	$ 56,000	20%
	Growth assets (stocks)	$ 11,200	4%
	Hard assets (home)	$112,000	40%
	Total	$280,000	100%

FINANCIAL PLAN #6 (Continued)

DEBT: 0

ANNUAL SAVING AMOUNT: 0

OTHER FUTURE INCOME: none

FINANCIAL GOALS (where she wants to be)

more income for comfortable retirement
others: travel and gifts to her family, occasional foreign tours

INVESTMENT STRATEGY (how to do it)

Like most people, she would like more income, but she is
meeting her present cost of living. No longer having mortgage
payments has helped her cash flow situation. Still, she feels that
she is living too close to the line, and more income would
help.

There are three reasonable ways she could increase her
income:

1. She could invest a greater percentage of her short-term
funds in longer-term securities. Half seems reasonable to her.
For the safety she demands, federally insured CDs and U.S.
Treasury obligations would be appropriate. Because she
doesn't trust long-term investments, she could only "go out" a
maximum of five years for a portion of the funds. The rest
could be positioned "short" with maturities of two years.

2. She could rent out a room in her large house. This would
provide her with income and company, but it doesn't appeal to
her right now. She agrees it's an idea for the future should a
compatible person come along. She likes having the house to
herself so her family can visit in comfort.

3. She could earn some money, perhaps, by tutoring. This
does appeal to her.

There is an inconsistency in this portfolio. The long-term
investments are not the quality or maturity of the other
investments. They are high-yield (meaning lower grade)
twenty- to thirty-year bonds. She has not dealt with the
significance of their potential risk as indicated both by quality
and maturity dates. She might sell these bonds and use the

proceeds to invest with her other funds. The loss of income from these high-yield bonds can be offset by increased income from her short-term securities extended to longer maturities. She would be invested with higher quality, and in a more flexible position should inflation increase in the future.

Finally, in reviewing her stock portfolio, it is noted that her inherited securities are too speculative for her situation and have no dividends. She decides to trade them for three high-quality issues, in different industries, all with solid dividends. This small stock portfolio plus the equity in her house represent some offset to the conservative income-producing assets that she needs to meet her living expenses.

12

Whatever You Say Is All Right

ABOUT INVESTMENT ADVISERS

MEN play the investment "game" to win. Yet if they lose, they take the consequences. Money is the point system—the great measure of success. Women investors, however, do not always approach investing this way. So when a woman seeks financial help, her expectations for good counsel may be different from her adviser's.

Teresa Trustful, fifty years old, unmarried and a modest wage-earner, took her recent $70,000 inheritance to a financial adviser recommended by a friend. The adviser considered himself an investment genius. He made his living by trading—buying and selling quickly to take advantage of short-term fluctuations in market prices—and used the same philosophy with his clients. The result: He put Teresa into speculative options and stocks. Teresa completely trusted her adviser, and did not understand the possible consequences.

Now it is five years later. Teresa, through the adviser, has lost much of the money. She doesn't know how much because she couldn't or wouldn't read the paperwork. Still, she tells me that she is willing "to take a little risk now and then." The adviser is still her broker. She says she basically doesn't like to deal with money, that she has too much responsibility in her life. The only reason she still has anything at all is that along the way, another friend advised her to buy a condo because apartment rents were rapidly increasing. The condo has appreciated significantly, and she has some safety for her future.

I'm not certain if this trader was aware of Teresa's circumstances, although he is legally required to know them and trade suitably. In his mind, I think he saw Teresa as "fair game." Her inheritance was his good fortune. A more conscientious adviser would have recognized that Teresa might never have such a large sum of money again in her life, that what she needed was security. This adviser might have recommended putting a down payment on a home and investing the rest in the bank, U.S. Treasury securities, or some high-quality bonds and stocks. The adviser's final action would be to tell her goodbye, except for a longer-term review.

Her portfolio might have looked like this:

$30,000 toward a condo of $100,000
$10,000 in an insured CD
$10,000 in an intermediate, government bond fund
$10,000 in an income-oriented stock fund
$10,000 in a growth stock fund

PROFESSIONAL HELP: WHEN AND WHO?

Up to now you have learned how, and why, to do your own financial planning—understanding the investment choices and deciding which investments suit your needs and which present an economic opportunity. Yet depending only on yourself has its limits, too. When should you turn to an experienced professional for help, and to which one?

Mary is forty, a single heiress with assets adequate for a comfortable middle-class life-style. She does not need to work, travels some, and enjoys herself. In the past, she had a professional career, and on her uncle's death managed the family business for a brief time. So she does understand basic business concepts and asks the right questions. Nevertheless . . .

Mary tells me that since most of her income (and her younger brother's) is now dependent on her investment portfolio, she has decided she can't do it herself. She needs someone to manage it for her, as her uncle always did. She believes her ability to hire someone to do it for her would undoubtedly get better results than she could by herself.

Currently, a friend, a former financial professional—who does not work either (Mary says he lives off his investments)—is her official investment adviser; for his management services she pays him an annual 3 percent of the value of her portfolio. They have no written contract. She has given him "discretion" on her behalf and her brother's, but not in writing. He places all investment orders for her with broker "friends" at major brokerage firms, telling Mary that they provide good information. For this she pays standard broker's commissions. (*Fact:* Most money managers get significant brokerage discounts.)

When I try to point out the potential problems of this arrangement and possible illegal abuse, Mary says, "He is making money for me."

I tell her, "That's good."

Mary continues, "Of course, everyone loses some money."

So I ask how much he is making. Mary has no idea. In fact, she doesn't know what her portfolio is worth or how to calculate its value. She holds her own securities, and therefore does not get monthly brokerage statements showing their value.

I recommend Mary do three things to learn how her adviser is really doing:

1. Find out what her securities are worth and what percentage increase is occurring each year—including interest, dividends, and capital gains. She knew their value at the time the estate was settled since the attorney provided those figures.

2. Compare this number with what she would have received over the same period from riskless investments, such as Treasury bills and insured bank certificates of deposit.

3. Compare the percentage of increase with the change in the Standard & Poor's stock market average over the same time period.

Her professional adviser should be able to give her those last two numbers or she might check back issues of *The Wall Street Journal* at the public library.

It turns out that when Mary's uncle's estate was settled, bonds had high yields and general stock prices were lower than at present. It was not magic management that increased the value of Mary's original portfolio. All she had to do was own the securities. The real measure of success would be how much the managed portfolio had increased compared to the averages.

Mary has agreed to do some calculations and begin to understand her own situation, even though it will be a lot of work. Whether her trust in her financial adviser is warranted I don't know. She certainly can afford the best in expert advice, along with timely market information.

*   *   *

Having someone help you and losing control are two different things. Good advice and information do not necessarily require total delegation of money management to the "experts." And sometimes, what I call "plain vanilla" investing is the best way to a successful portfolio. Complicated investments requiring a major educational effort and frequent trading may not perform any better than the old reliables—stocks, corporate bonds, municipal bonds, government paper, bank accounts, and real estate.

A WORD ABOUT WINDFALLS

But what if you have a lot of assets? Have you suddenly inherited more money than you are used to, as in Mary's case? Or have half of the proceeds from a postdivorce house sale? Don't be intimidated by money. You *don't* have to rush out and hire a money manager. Your new asset may be no different from the smaller sum with which you are used to dealing. It may just have more zeros on the right-hand side!

More money does not always mean more individual investments—what the professionals call "positions." And diversification—a good strategy for protection—doesn't mean you buy everything you hear about. A portfolio of ten to twenty positions is plenty to follow. And there's no rush. You don't always need to be seriously invested for the long term. A low profile in liquid, safe, interest-bearing securities and bank accounts will keep your principal intact while earning steady money. This may not be exciting or your ultimate goal, but you won't lose in the meantime.

More money shouldn't change your basic approach toward it. You still follow the same financial planning and evaluation process you have already learned in this book:

- *Set goals.* They may be easier to reach with more money, or you may "up the ante" and find more challenging goals.

- Find out *what you own* (count it), and what you *spend and save* (this may be a longer list).
- *Know your situation.* You may now have more taxes to consider.
- Shop from the same list of *investment possibilities.* Only maybe now you can afford some new ones, too.
- *Monitor* your investments periodically, even if you now have the best professional advice money can buy.
- And finally, *keep records,* in a bigger filing cabinet, perhaps.

Inheriting money is one way to get rich, easier than some. Managing a sudden jackpot is not an occasion for panic. Enjoy the control and investigate the choices open to you, but with the same basic financial planning method as always. If you decide to seek investment expertise or general financial help, I recommend that you first do your own financial outline and some serious thinking about your goals. It will help the professional to help you.

BEFORE YOU SELECT A PROFESSIONAL

You do not "need" to become an investment expert, any more than you "need" to become a lawyer, accountant, physician, or car mechanic. Housekeeper, mother, career woman, and sex symbol may be enough!

Having a consultant who specializes in finance, works at it all the time, and is in touch with ongoing developments and opinion can be a great help. Especially if you do not choose to devote a major amount of time to the subject. But before you decide to see a financial specialist, be aware of two things: first, the specialist's expectations and responsibilities, and second, your expectations and responsibilities.

THE SPECIALISTS

No one works for nothing. Everyone expects to be paid. Do you understand how your professional advisers are paid?

This is important to know when determining which professionals to hire, when, and what interests they might have in certain investment products.

Attorneys and *accountants* usually receive an hourly fee—more time is more money—and talk *is* expensive. So before you hire one, ask, "How much?" You also need to find out if the fee is within a reasonable range for someone in your situation. Sometimes attorneys and accountants offer other services for profit, such as estate and financial planning. Nothing is wrong with paying for service well performed. With legal and accounting advice, if you need it and it is done right, it is worthwhile.

You should certainly consult an attorney when you need legal advice. This includes situations that are obvious, such as a lawsuit as well as preparatory work for limiting risk of potential problems. But estate planning, remarriage, setting up a business, considering a divorce may also call for legal advice ahead of time.

A good accountant will not only help you prepare tax forms, she or he may save you money because of expertise in tax law. A knowledgeable accountant can help you plan for future tax years and show you how to set up proper bookkeeping for personal use or a new business.

Keep in mind that an accountant's approach is generally toward saving on taxes rather than investing to make money. Neither an accountant nor an attorney are necessarily investment experts, and their financial opinion may not be suitable for your personal goals. Successful professionals who invest their own money often have financial opinions reflecting their own circumstances.

If you are getting investment advice from an attorney or accountant, check to be certain that there is no conflict of interest on their part. Specifically, does the professional receive additional remuneration if you purchase a recommended investment? How much? Or is this recommendation part of the "old boy network," the way of doing business where customers are passed on and favors repaid. If this is the case, you must judge if you still think the advice is correct and know how it compares to alternatives. You still have to do your homework. Yes, some attorneys and accountants sell more than traditional professional services. Some sell financial plans and/or investments.

Like having a good doctor on hand before you get sick, it is a good idea to know a good attorney and a good accountant should you need them. Referrals from people you respect always help. Ask why this person is specifically recommended, and what are her or his strengths and weaknesses. You must judge the referral yourself, of course, because the expert has to be someone with whom you feel comfortable, someone who can relate to your needs.

Financial advisers come in a great variety in today's financial marketplace. Banks, brokerage firms, insurance companies, financial planners all solicit you for investment money. Taking care of your money is very profitable. Just look at all the expensive advertising in the media competing for your attention.

The person who used to be called a "stockbroker" is now called a "financial consultant," "account executive," and "vice-president of investments." (I prefer the general term: "investment broker.") This is because stockbrokers no longer just trade stocks. Some of the newer brokers don't even know much about individual stock issues, or how to read financial statements. They are taught to sell corporate-favored products.

I remember a new broker trainee, just back from training at the head office of her brokerage firm, who was assigned to "cold call" a minimum of forty prospects per day (or night). She was soliciting prospective investors for the firm's mutual funds. She yelled from her desk, "I've got one; she's got money." This is known as "dial and smile." It amazes me how many people will invest thousands of dollars over the phone without asking many questions. I expect that same investor would agonize much longer over buying a new washing machine.

The greatest advantages to using an investment broker with a large firm are access to information and access to a broad spectrum of investments. Brokerage "houses" like to consider themselves "supermarkets" for investments so that whatever you need, they have it. However, they do not have a full range of insurance products (and often experience) or real estate properties for single individual purchase. And you may prefer real estate that you select and manage yourself, as opposed to a limited partnership, for example, which is available through a brokerage house.

Brokers are paid on commission. The more they buy and sell, the more money they make. Different investments, or "products" as they are called, provide different commissions. Most brokerage firms pay more to brokers to sell their "in-house" or proprietary products—mutual funds and certain limited partnerships, for instance. Less liquid investments, such as limited partnerships, pay the biggest commissions on the theory that the broker is "locking up" some trading money and should be compensated accordingly.

Brokers are paid to know what is going on in the markets. The computer gives them current information, "the tapes," which show trades on the exchanges; individual stocks and bonds; and other important financial data. The broker's recommendations may depend on her or his ability to assess market action and use the opinions of the firm's experts. It is difficult to define what a "good" broker is before seeing results. (As in a beauty shop, you don't know how a new hair style is going to look when the stylist begins to cut.) But here are some hints.

Good brokers:

- Take the time to understand their clients' needs and risk levels
- Appraise market conditions wisely and judge financial products accordingly
- Pay attention to details and are well organized
- Are usually experienced
- Are able to communicate with you
- Are knowledgeable and provide factual information
- Are candid and truthful, and find the right investment for you without regard to commissions

You must judge the broker for honesty and ability. As mentioned, referrals are a way to begin your search. Sometimes it is a good idea to talk with the manager of the brokerage office first to get the name of a broker who would be appropriate for you, but in the end, it is still your appraisal that counts. Even with a good broker, keep tight control over your decisions and your financial planning, and monitor the results.

Predictions are not good information. I once overheard a broker tell his client, "Now Harriet, we'll buy the stock and sell when it [the famous stock market index] reaches 1330. [It was then at 1280.] When the Dow gets up there, some will think it's going to 1370. It won't. We'll sell then."

How does he know all this? From God's mouth to his ear? Though a typical brokerish attitude, which he may actually believe, it isn't fact. (*Fact:* In the summer of 1987, the Dow went to the 2500s.) What he stated was his hunch, and superstition-prone minds sometimes forget the difference. Later, he probably forgot and denied his statement. Remember: You are allowed to say "no" to your adviser's opinion. Replying "whatever you say" is not all right.

Financial advisers are increasingly available at *banks,* which frequently offer trading at discount prices in stocks and bonds and, of course, promote bank accounts, certificates of deposit, and other bank products. Some sell stock in their own bank. Bank services vary, so find out for yourself exactly what is offered and at what cost. Generally, larger accounts and trusts held at the bank get more personal guidance, but banks are giving more training to employees who assist investors in buying and selling in the stock and bond markets.

Bank professionals are usually on salary, though sometimes they get bonuses or other incentives for increasing business. Because the bank's investment adviser is not motivated by commission, and because of the traditional conservative stance of many banks, you can generally expect less aggressive trading recommendations. The investment experience of the personnel, your need for personal guidance, and the bank's investment services are what must be considered when choosing a bank for your investment account.

Discount brokerage firms are becoming very popular because of their low prices and increasing range of services. Their salaried personnel will trade most securities for you and many also sell mutual funds. Discount brokers do not provide personal investment advice, though. If you don't need the guidance, this may please you—no sales solicitations and bargain prices. Opening an account is the same as at a standard brokerage firm.

Some limited possibilities exist for making investments without brokers. Federal Reserve Banks sell U.S. Treasury securities directly to the public. Many mutual funds sell and redeem their own units. But for the most part, stocks, bonds, variations thereof, and partnerships are not available directly. You need a broker to make most investments.

MONEY MANAGERS

If you are very rich, you may be able to find and afford the very best professional advisers. Small mistakes are affordable. But big mistakes, and misjudgments about the people you are trusting, can be more costly and sometimes ruinous. *Money managers* "run money," as they say, for big accounts. This may be on a personal basis or in a "pool." Your pension plan at work may be managed this way. Selection of a money manager must include track record, the management reputation, and area of specialization. Some are set up to be more conservative than others, but most do specialize in some direction. You must find one to match your needs. Referrals from a brokerage firm or bank may be a source for contact, but watch out for vested interests, recommendations only for their own managers. Fees are usually calculated as a percentage of portfolio value, some variation related to performance or a combination. This may be cost effective for a large account because commissions are greatly reduced for order size. The hitch is that you need a large sum to invest. Hiring a money manager is not a guarantee of superior performance.

If you are not rich, you might not be able to hire the expensive specialist or wish to pay high brokerage commissions. In that case, as with home remodeling, shop around, do more of the work yourself, and buy the best advice in your price range. Mutual funds are another way to hire a money manager, but there is no personal contact involved— the pool of client money invested in the fund becomes the large sum for investment.

FINANCIAL SPECIALISTS—INSURANCE AND REAL ESTATE

Insurance brokers or agents sell a range of insurance products designed to protect your interests, to help toward retirement and estate planning. *Real estate brokers* and agents sell real estate. Both are commissioned sales and both often have added incentives of contests and trips.

You may be in the market for one of these products, and

it certainly makes sense to see an expert when you know what you want. But don't go to a specialist for general investment advice and expect to receive unbiased recommendations. Specialists are trained to understand their products, and tend to see what they sell as the answer to all your needs.

Real estate salespersons would be hard pressed to find a more superior investment than real estate, regardless of how the market looks. Insurance salespersons have the same approach. Not everyone needs life insurance and not everyone needs it throughout her or his life.

In looking for a specialist, be a comparison shopper. Don't feel you must be loyal because the professional is a relative or friend. You need to understand what they sell, and then gather competitive information.

FINANCIAL PLANNERS

Financial planner is a term that includes everybody: brokers, bankers, insurance and real estate salespersons, maybe even your father-in-law. Titles such as "certified financial planner" mean completion of a course on financial planning. Generally, there is little government regulation of financial planners, regardless of title.

Some financial planners work as a team: the lawyer, the accountant, and the financial expert. Consulting with such a group can be a good idea, particularly if you have very complicated affairs, which does not always equate with having a lot of money—just because you have a lot of money does not mean you must have a financial planner. Qualifications of the professional, costs, and the products they sell, if any, are still what counts. Many financial planners charge a fee to do a plan and then sell you financial products. Sometimes they recommend another firm that does the selling, but they may be associated with this other firm or even own it under a separate corporate structure. In general, the products they sell you are far more profitable than the initial cost of the financial plan. Real estate and insurance professionals frequently do financial planning and want to sell you their own products. Many financial planners have access to a broad range of products, so they can place your money in appropriate investment vehicles. The financial planner's ability to discern good investments to meet your needs is as important as the ability to plan tax strategy and recommend cash management techniques.

I am a strong advocate of the financial planning process, as you know from this book, but I am concerned about the growing development of financial planning as a tool to help the salesperson rather than the investor. This is why I urge you to learn how to do the basics yourself. What to buy may be the bottom line of a financial plan, and you don't necessarily want to limit your choice to what the planner sells.

A limited number of financial planners just do the financial plan. They don't sell anything. These people are often tax attorneys or accountants with specialized expertise. They tend to be costly, but if you need their help, it may be worth the expense.

YOU AND THE FINANCIAL EXPERT

The services of a financial professional include: (1) providing you with current and accurate information; (2) sometimes executing your order to buy or sell and providing related service; and (3) sometimes giving you advice and opinions. A pleasant bedside manner may be nice, but it's secondary to the job.

Some of my female clients have told me that their prior investment advisers were like their "own sons" or "best friends." This is usually an illusion. Advice may be as good as the adviser's ability, but it is *your* decision; it's still your money (as in your liability, your tax return, your body, your car).

You should know what is in your best interest—that is your job. If you have used the process of financial planning and understand the framework of reference for investing, you won't have to turn over your decision-making to others.

Knowing when to trust the investment information you get is difficult, but the right questions and a businesslike discussion will help.

It is perfectly true in the investment world that a professional adviser benefits from, and is entitled to, some correct information about your needs and financial abilities. But your privacy should also be a consideration. You do not necessarily need to "get undressed" or tell all—as is often said. A request for more details can be just another sales technique to find out how much you have and what your "hot button" (what you will buy) is. How much to tell, and to whom, is your decision, not an automatic response.

Use your judgment, as you would when shopping for a car, washing machine, or computer. You need more than a good salesperson. You need someone who is reliable for future service.

Finally, in addition to the qualifications of potential advisers, be aware of the governmental regulatory bodies that govern their actions (or in some cases, do not govern). If things are not going right and you cannot get action with assertive and reasonable requests, governmental agencies may be your best bet. The office manager in your financial institution should be your first step. But the appropriate government agency is the next.

To summarize: Financial specialists are selling. You are

buying. Your business is to decide the

Purpose of the purchase,
Price suitable to value,
Service needed,
Products of choice, and
Quality.

Realize that finance is Big Business. The industry's goal is to make a profit. To be a wise consumer in a competitive financial market, be informed and conduct business in a reasonable, businesslike manner—but be protective of your own interests.

CHAPTER

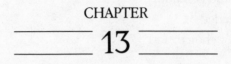

13

Be Prepared

A DISASTER PLAN FOR THE UNPREPARED WOMAN

A desperate woman calls me at the office. Her husband, a client, does all their investing, but he is ill. She tells me that she is "so sorry to do this," but she needs to have some of their money market funds. She is taking over for him at this time, and really needs the money to remodel her kitchen. She begs, would I please send her the money, and she hopes she can "put it back soon."

Permission granted.

Did you ever wonder why the course called "Home Economics" is not about money?

No one gets married thinking they might get divorced. No one really expects the death of a spouse when it happens. We are not usually ready for these disruptions. Sometimes life circumstances change our plans, just when we think we have it all working smoothly. Divorce and death are difficult enough without the added weight of financial stress. Home economics courses that teach cooking and sewing are of little help when you are on your own and know little about your own money.

Many such financial problems can be eased if you and your husband normally share in the knowledge, decisions, and responsibility of managing your money. Unfortunately, many marriages do not operate this way. The traditional arrangement still seems to be more usual: the husband managing the investments and the wife signing the tax form.

To put yourself in the best possible position for an emergency change in life circumstances, you must know essentially everything you would need to know if you were on your own. Knowledge is power over your own life. And you can start gaining it by applying the financial planning outline described in this book.

To prepare for any unexpected emergency:

• You need to know what you *own* and *owe.* You need to know if these assets are titled in joint name, individually, or in trust. Don't forget assets like life insurance and pension plans. Who owns these and who the beneficiary is are important (beneficiaries can be changed).

• You need to know your *income,* individually and jointly. This would include earnings from work as well as other income, such as dividends, interest, rents, business income, and pensions. Also, note potential income from pension plans, inheritances, and trusts.

• Don't forget *expenses.* This is a good time to figure out just what it costs to live. Include your tax liabilities.

• You need to be clear on your *financial goals* and concerns as well as those of your spouse.

• You should have a list of the *professional advisers* you use and how to reach them: attorney, accountant, insurance agents, banker, investment broker, household and auto experts, and any others.

• You need to know where all *records* and vital documents are kept and how they are organized.

If all things are going well between the two of you, this information should be easy to get. And if you're following the advice in this book, you have already begun organizing it and writing it all down in your notebook. This may also be a good time to initiate a discussion of goals and planning.

If this presents a problem for you, and you recognize that you might need a "disaster plan," consider the following: *Almost everything financial shows up on your tax return.* You sign this document, and therefore you should not only read it but have access to a copy of each year's return. Your income shows on the return. Profits and losses from sales reveal ownership. Interest-bearing debts should be there, too. Most income-producing and depreciable assets are there. Corporations and trusts must also file returns.

Become acquainted with other records as well: mortgages, wills, deeds, pension plan descriptions, insurance policies, bank and brokerage account statements, records of the cost of your assets, Social Security numbers, other vital certificates. Photocopy the important ones for your notebook.

Secrets. Income from nonregistered, tax-free bonds, the ones with the coupons to be cut, may not be declared on tax forms. Securities can be stacked away in an office safe or lock box. Business interests can sometimes be hidden, although it is more difficult. Assets acquired that produce no income or losses do not show on a tax return until sold and declared. Stocks without dividends, gold, silver, and collectibles can be private. A number of my male clients have even requested that brokerage statements and phone calls go only to their offices so their wives have no idea of even the name of the brokerage house with which they do business.

Work benefits, such as pension plans, profit-sharing arrangements, and insurance are often unclear, even to the owner/beneficiary. This may be a good time to clarify all these benefits for planning purposes.

If you know what income is made, and how it is spent and saved, the numbers should match.

QUESTIONS TO ASK YOURSELF

Upon divorce or death, what assets would be yours?

What liabilities?

What would you have for income? How about earnings, interest, dividends, rents, alimony, child support?

If you will need more income, do you need more education now to improve your earning ability?

If you are alone at retirement age, what would you have for income?

Do you have emergency cash in your own name?

Are you aware of your state's property laws, divorce laws (and typical settlements), and estate tax laws? Don't get misinformation from friends. If necessary, see an attorney, even at a preliminary stage of planning.

Determining all these numbers is not difficult if you gather the facts. The outline you need is in this book. If you know this information, you will have no financial surprises. Your future will be more in your own control.

You have the tools for making your financial decisions and now is the time to begin to do so. Remember: Financial decisions are only as good as the life context into which you put them. You must decide for yourself what it is that makes your life significant. You must determine your goals and know what your finances permit; it's the only way you can move out of dependency and toward self-direction. And, after all, isn't that what money is for?

AFTERWORD

My Personal Investment Philosophy

AS a woman, I, too, identify with an attitude of conservative investing. I think we all worry a little about falling through the crack, slipping from secure career woman to bag lady!

I am married again, and my husband and I separate our assets into mine, his, and ours. We like to spend and invest independently, although there are areas of joint financial interest and decision-making.

My definition of conservative includes investing significantly in growth as well as backup savings of "mattress money." But this stance does not preclude occasional, carefully considered risk. I take risks that have good chances of success but *only* with assets I can afford to lose. I do not speculate just for the game—and I do less speculating now than when I first became a broker, which is typical of people with experience in the market.

I consider myself to be conservative because my first concern is to protect the capital that protects my long-term security. In addition to preserving my capital, I expect my assets to increase in real value, but I am content to accept a reasonable market rate under most circumstances. Even with my brokering experience, I do not consider myself a "wise woman" who can outsmart everyone else.

I am aware that past performance has shown that low-risk investments producing straight interest income have not been sufficient to offset inflation, so I position the major part of my assets in growth investments. I bought intermediate length bonds when the interest rates were attractive, but even then I was not willing to risk long-term (twenty- to thirty-year) paper for a slightly higher return. I am on my guard to monitor these income investments and constantly remind myself to sell should interest rates begin to reverse significantly.

I believe in diversification. It feels better because the future is unknown. Diversification does not necessarily mean a little of everything, a smorgasbord of the entire spectrum. It means putting together a plan that builds positions in investments of my choice. The amount of money in each investment may vary with my needs and my judgment about its economic value at the time.

Saving is one of my habits. Even when I was earning my first career dollars, I managed to put a little of every paycheck into the bank. The first car I bought was paid for in full with these savings and a trade-in. It felt good to do this without debt.

I always feel a need for an emergency cash fund. This might be in a money market fund, U.S. Treasury bill, or federally insured bank account. I think that my comfort level requires an absolute minimum of ready cash, beyond a normal monthly expense allotment, in the range of $10,000. It could be more if I were saving for a specific purpose, in a spending mode, or felt that it was time to tread water between investments and be in cash.

It is my prejudice to own a house. I can think of reasons

why home ownership is not always desirable or necessary, but now that I'm past the age of forty-five it just feels right. Fixing the cost of a major expense for the rest of my life seems like good planning. Even a slow, creeping inflation will eventually catch up with our assets, or, in a "worst case" scenario such as a major depression, everything may become devalued, but at least you can live in a house. This doesn't mean buy at any price, at any time, anywhere. You still have to "buy right"—that is, on terms with which you can live. I am in favor of low leverage, as small a mortgage as possible, for this purpose.

Even though current tax laws encourage borrowing for your home, I think the risk of high leverage belongs outside of my security base. The real estate purchase need not be one to live in. It could be "a substitute property," one to offset renting because it is a better location of choice.

After cash and savings (which includes my short- and intermediate-income securities) and real estate, funding and investing in my retirement fund and appropriate insurance to protect the assets are next on my list for a conservative, protective strategy.

With this security in place, I want to own some stocks. Some are held in my IRA, but since the change in the tax laws I am not currently adding growth stock positions here. Why give up the liquidity for penalties on early withdrawal? Stock appreciation has no taxable effect until sale, and tax on sales may be as low now as when I retire. If I were investing for income, the IRA protection would still make sense.

My strategy in stocks is generally to buy for long-term prospects. I watch my portfolio to see if performance is as expected, and I don't hesitate to trade when I change my mind.

Although I recognize that not everyone is comfortable in selecting a portfolio, it is my approach. My primary reason for buying a particular stock is that it fits into *my perception of market trends and economic cycles.* I come to this perception mainly by reading world and financial news and opinions. I then compare the company with others in its field. The important factors here are earning capability, cash flow position, debt structure, valuable assets, and management reputation. (Financial reports are easier to read if you mentally deduct some of the zeros and compare them to running a household.) Sometimes I call the company, the "shareholder information" service, to ask questions and hear what the company is saying about itself. I also give some weight to certain ethical considerations.

I am a bit of a "contrarian" (just ask my mother), buying what's out of favor and waiting. If you are hoping that I am finally getting to my market prediction that will make you rich, you are out of luck. I don't do that. You have to take that responsibility for yourself. After all, you may be smarter than I am!

I try to be in control of my financial situation. I review my investment portfolio, and I assess—by performance and by percentages—each kind of investment: cash, fixed income, stocks, real estate, collectibles, business enterprise, or speculation. Too many positions are difficult to track. Fifteen stock positions are a maximum monitoring job for me. (Starting out with even one stock position is certainly okay if your safety assets are in place. A minimum for buying one stock or mutual fund might be $2,500.)

I simplify. One of the goals of my life is to make the nitty-gritty easier so that I can concentrate on other things. I avoid fancy, complex investments that are not easily understood. Are there too many caveats? Is there too much legal jargon? Unclear "what if's"? In these cases, I pass. I like to understand what I am buying so that I can weigh the probable success or failure. I don't like to rely solely on someone else's opinion.

I am cost aware. I don't like to pay too many extra fees because the investment must then compensate in performance for the heavy "load."

I try to use common sense. What *feels right* to me when I think it through, probably is right. I like to believe that women are particularly good at common sense because of our practical experience in managing the necessities of everyday life. So I just remind myself to apply it to my finances. Decisions become much easier.

I am always concerned with timing, identifying opportunities and acting on them. It is as important as the investment choice. It is the major reason people make money. *When* you buy your house may be as important as where it is. *When* you buy a stock or bond determines profit. Sometimes it is wise to wait for the right opportunity.

Finally, control over my assets is very important to me. I want to be the decision-maker, the manager. Keeping good records becomes essential. Most important, I take charge of the decisions by understanding and *making plans.* I am not always successful, but I make decisions that are appropriate for me.

What is right for me may not be for you. But I have shared the information and my personal thoughts with you in the hope that you will no longer need to be dependent on anyone for your future security. You can have a new freedom. The most important lesson of this book is that you are responsible for your own security. Regardless of whether you have an adviser to help, your future depends on *your* understanding, *your* attitude, and *your* participation in making and acting upon the financial plan that is right for you.

GLOSSARY

ACCRUED INTEREST Accumulated interest on a bond due to the holder of the bond. On sale of a bond, the seller is entitled to all interest from the last payment date up until sale date. The purchaser remits this amount on purchase to the prior owner. On payment date, the bond's agent bank will pay the new owner of record (or coupon holder) a full six months' interest. Stock dividends do not pay this way. You either own the stock on dividend date or you don't.

ANNUITIES/TSA Created by insurance companies, tax-sheltered annuities are savings investments in which income compounds tax-deferred. Annuities, like insurance, have beneficiaries and avoid probate. To annuitize means to take periodic payout over a scheduled period. A fixed annuity pays a fixed rate of interest, while a variable annuity has an uncertain rate of return based on how the monies are invested. Nonprofit organizations (schools, hospitals) have special annuity programs with an extra tax benefit: They are deducted from earnings as well as providing tax-deferred income.

APPRECIATION An increase in value.

BALLOON PAYMENT LOANS Loans that require most of the payment on maturity; these are usually short-term loans.

BEAR/BULL Wall Street slang. A bear is a pessimist who sells her holdings because she believes their value will decline. A bull is an optimist who buys because she believes the value of her holdings will increase. A bear market is a declining market; a bull market is a rising one.

BID/ASK A proposal to buy a security at a specific price and an offer to sell a security at a specific price. The difference is called the "spread."

BLUE-CHIP STOCK Stock of the highest-quality companies with a long history of profits and dividend payments. They are so-called because, in poker, the blue chips have the highest value.

BOND, NOTE, DEBENTURE A debt obligation of the issuer, it is a contract that states the amount borrowed (face or par), when it must be paid (maturity), and how much the interest (coupon) is. These securities are marketable. If issued by a corporation, the interest is taxable. If issued by a state, municipality, or government entity, the interest is tax-free federally and may be free of state and/or local tax. The interest rate is usually lower for municipal bonds than for corporate bonds.

CALL FEATURE A statement on a bond that elaborates on the terms of the issuer's right to recall the bond at a specified price on certain dates.

CAPITAL GAIN/LOSS Tax terminology for profit or loss on capital or investment items, which include real estate, stocks, bond values (not interest), business interests, collectibles.

CASH EQUIVALENTS These are short-term investments, usually low-risk, that can be quickly converted to cash. They include demand deposits at banks, money market funds, U.S. Treasury bills, etc.

CDs Certificates of Deposit are issued by banks and pay a specified interest rate until a specified maturity date, ranging from three months to several years; a penalty is usually charged for early withdrawal.

COLLECTIBLES Investments in nonfinancial goods that are valued in a restricted market of devotees, including precious metals, antiques, rugs, paintings, jewelry, stamps, etc.

COMMISSION Charge or fee for the purchase of an investment from brokerage firms, real estate firms, insurance companies, mutual funds, limited partnerships, it is sometimes called "the load" that can be charged "up front" when you buy the investment, at the end when you sell, or both ways.

COMMODITY FUTURE A contract to buy or sell a certain commodity—such as gold, wheat, or bonds—at some future time at a fixed price. Speculators trade commodities by putting up a small percentage of the contract value as "good faith money." This leverage makes for high risk.

COMMODITY OPTIONS The further leverage of commodity contracts through the use of options, which require less cash per contract than the commodity contract itself.

COMMON STOCK Also known as equity, common stock gives an investor ownership in a corporation with the attendant risk/reward prospects.

COMPOUNDING The process of interest earning interest.

COST BASIS Original cost including commissions of an investment, with important meaning for calculating tax consequences on the sale of the investment.

COUPON BONDS Unregistered bonds (no ownership name printed on them), which have coupons attached, representing demand payment to the bearer of such coupons. These are also known as "bearer bonds" and are no longer issued by the U.S. government or municipalities. Older issues still trade.

DEPRECIATION A loss of value. Investment real estate, buildings, and equipment are said to be "losing value" as they get older; to offset this loss they are permitted certain tax benefits—even if, in fact, they are worth more.

DISCOUNT The amount bonds are discounted or reduced in value from par in the marketplace to account for an unfavorable change in interest rates, except when newly issued below par value. Cost basis affects taxable profit and loss.

DIVERSIFICATION Spreading your investment dollars among different investments to moderate risk.

DIVIDEND Stocks and mutual funds pay out a portion of earnings in dividends—fully taxable. Dollar amounts vary according to the financial status of the company and its desire to reinvest or pay out profits. It is usually paid quarterly.

DOW JONES INDUSTRIAL AVERAGE Thirty blue-chip industrial stocks that have long been regarded as the chief indicator of health of the market.

EQUITY Ownership of anything, but often used as a substitute for the word *stock*.

FLOAT "The float" refers to the number of shares issued by a company. It can also refer to interest rates that "float" or change with the times, and are generally pegged to some short-term investment vehicle.

GINNY MAE The slang name for the Government National Mortgage Association, abbreviated as GNMA. This agency buys home mortgages with thirty-year maturities, guarantees the repayment of principal and interest, and resells them in pools. They are brokered in lots of $25,000 or in unit trusts and mutual funds. Since mortgages are paid off at undetermined times (on the sale of a house), GNMAs do not have a fixed maturity. For this reason their yields are not calculated in the same way as other bonds and may be misleading. This calculation is based on current yield and does not account for any maturity or even an "average life"—said to be about twelve years.

GOOD-UNTIL-CANCELED An order to buy or sell a security beyond the market day until you give further notice. It is a binding contract at whatever your stated terms until canceled.

GROWTH STOCK Stock of companies that reinvest profit to maximize their potential. Typically, there are no dividends or low dividends paid out to the stockholder.

HIGH-YIELD BOND Also known as a "junk bond," it is a lower-quality, noninvestment-grade security sometimes floated so the issuer can borrow money for corporate "takeovers." They pay higher interest to offset the higher risk.

INDEX OPTION An option on a variety of indexes, permitting speculation and "hedging" or guarding of risk on market

swings. Indexes exist for the Dow Jones Industrial Average, the
Standard & Poor's Average, as well as on separate industry
composites, such as the energy group, the utilities, etc.

INTEREST Bonds and bank investments pay out interest as "rent"
for the use of the lender's money. Bond interest is usually paid
twice a year at a specified amount and may be taxable or
tax-free, depending on the status of the issuer.

IRA/KEOGH Individual Retirement Accounts and KEOGHs are
retirement plans that allow deductions and defer taxes on the
investment income until the money is withdrawn. IRAs were
originally set up by the government to permit most wage
earners to invest $2,000 a year and take a full deduction, but
deductions are now severely restricted. KEOGHs were set up
for the self-employed and their employees and still have some
tax advantages, though they have also been limited.

INFLATION A process of increasing prices usually accompanied
by an expansion in paper money and credit. Investments with
fixed returns suffer under these conditions, while investments
that can grow with the expansion do better.

JOINT TENANTS WITH RIGHT OF SURVIVORSHIP Joint ownership or title to securities, allowing for equal rights and for
surviving parties to receive the entire property. This title may
avoid probate.

LEVERAGE An investment stance in which smaller dollars control
a large investment usually through the mechanism of borrowing. Leverage magnifies profit and loss and therefore carries a
higher risk.

LIMIT ORDER An order to sell a security at a specified price.

LIMITED PARTNERSHIP A legal structure for the pooling of
money in a partnership. The general partner manages the
business affairs; the limited partners are passive investors with
liability limited to the extent of their investment. This form of
investing was used extensively in the past for tax shelters.

LIQUIDITY Refers to the ability to quickly cash in an investment.
Cash equivalents are thought of as the most liquid, with least
chance of loss of any value. Stocks and bonds are also referred
to as liquid in that they, too, can be cashed in quickly. Real

estate, business interests, and collectibles are not considered liquid assets.

MARGIN Money borrowed by a customer against the collateral of her security account, usually to purchase an investment. Interest is charged on the amount borrowed.

MARKET VALUE The price at which a security can be bought or sold at a given time.

MONEY MARKET FUND A mutual fund invested in short-term government securities, certificates of deposit, and commercial paper; usually liquid; rates fluctuate daily.

MUNICIPAL BOND A bond issued by a government entity of a state or municipality. They are mostly tax-free as a federal concession to allow these government bodies to raise money at a lower rate of interest. New tax regulations limit the issuing of certain types of municipal bonds and the tax-deductibility of others.

MUTUAL FUND An investment company that combines the funds of many investors to buy a diversified portfolio managed by professionals. The objectives of the fund may vary—for example, income, growth, tax protection. The fund is issued in shares and pays dividends.

NET ASSET VALUE The NAV is the value of each share of a mutual fund at the close of a trading day, as calculated by the combined value of all its assets. It is also the "bid" price at which you could sell.

NET WORTH The value of your assets minus your liabilities.

ODD LOT In stock trades, less than 100 shares.

OPTION The right to buy, *a call option,* or sell, *a put option,* a security by a set time for a set amount, for which a premium is paid by the seller of the option. Options can be bought or sold on a variety of stocks, indexes, real estate, and commodities. They work as substitutes for stock but with more leverage because they cost less. There are many option strategies that serve different investment purposes.

OVER-THE-COUNTER Markets made for securities outside regular exchanges, such as the New York Stock Exchange or the American Stock Exchange. Individual dealers specialize in certain stocks and bonds, usually (but not always) those less traded than exchange stocks. The most traded issues are usually listed on the NASDAQ Exchange, but smaller capitalized issues can be found in the directory of dealers and current prices, called "the pink sheets."

P/E RATIO This is a ratio of the price of a stock to its earnings. It is a popular way to measure stocks selling at different prices. In this way comparisons among stocks in the same industry under the same market conditions are possible.

PAR VALUE The face value of a bond, usually $1,000 per bond. Quoted at 100, which means 100 percent of par.

PENNY STOCK Very speculative stocks, usually selling under $1 per share.

PORTFOLIO An itemized list of all security positions, whether for personal records or those of a mutual fund.

PREFERRED STOCK A class of stock that has a prior claim to dividends before common stock, but after bonds. It usually has a fixed dividend amount.

PREMIUM The amount a bond is marked up or increased in value from its par value in the marketplace, except when newly issued. The cost basis is what counts here for tax purposes.

PRIME RATE The rate charged by banks to their best customers for borrowing. It is a key indicator for investors concerned with the rise and fall of interest rates.

PRINCIPAL Your capital.

PROSPECTUS A legally required document offered to the investor by the issuer of a new security or mutual fund in which the financial structure of the company and its business objectives are described in detail. A prospectus must include information as to investment risk and conflicts of interest, if any.

PUT BOND Bonds with a special provision that the bond holder may "put back" the bond to the issuer at par prior to maturity on certain dates as stated on the contract.

QUOTE The price of a security when asked for by an investor or security trader, traditionally based on 100 shares of stock, or a $10,000 face-value bond. The investor may ask for both the "bid" and the "ask" if she wishes to see the spread.

RATING Bonds (and other securities) are measured as to their quality. Moody's and Standard & Poor's are two well-known rating services that are respected by investors. These services evaluate debt coverage, earnings, etc. of the issuer. Generally, higher-rated bonds pay less interest than low-rated bonds.

ROUND LOT In U.S. stocks, this means 100 shares, a customary unit of trade.

RULE OF 72 A simplified formula that allows a calculation to determine how long it would take a sum of money to double at a given rate of return: divide the rate of return into 72. It also is useful in calculating the effects of inflation on your money.

SECOND TRUST DEED An interest-bearing note with due date backed directly by real estate, but second to the interests of the first mortgage holder.

SETTLEMENT DATE The contractual date on which securities are to be paid for, or delivered as the result of sale. Stocks and bonds settle in five business days, special "cash settlements" and Treasury bills in one day, new issues by issuer declaration.

STOCK SPLIT An increase (or decrease with a reverse stock split) in the number of shares and a new price per share that is mathematically proportional to the split equation. A stock split does not increase the value per share.

STOP ORDER Instructions to your broker to sell or buy a security at your specified price or when it goes through that price. A *stop limit* order will only allow its sale or purchase at that exact price. If your intent is protection of loss, a stop limit may not work since your exact price might be bypassed.

STREET NAME A term meaning your securities are held in the name of the firm where you do your business rather than in your name. You may request that your securities be held in your own name whether you "take delivery" of them or leave them with the firm "in safe-keeping."

TAX BRACKET The percentage paid in taxes on the last dollars of your income. The new tax law designates two brackets: 15 percent and 28 percent.

TAX DEDUCTION Expenses that are allowed in order to reduce taxable income.

TAX-DEFERRED Income that is nontaxable until sale of an appreciated capital item, such as real estate, stocks, and bonds. Increased value of IRA and KEOGH plans are also tax-deferred until the money is taken out of the plan.

TENANT IN COMMON Title which is held so that each owner owns a specified proportionate share of the property. Upon death, the decedent's share is disposed of as her or his property alone.

TREASURY BILL, NOTE, BOND Debt instruments issued and guaranteed by the U.S. government. The interest is taxed federally, but is not taxable to the states. These are marketable securities without penalty on sale. The bills are three months to one year in maturity, and are bought at a discount to par. The difference represents the interest due on maturity. Notes are one to ten years in length, while bonds are ten years or more. Both pay interest twice a year.

TRUST A legal entity in which property is held by a trustee for the benefit of a designated person(s). In a "living trust" a person is sometimes her own trustee.

UNIT TRUST A security that combines the funds of many to buy a specified, closed portfolio, usually bonds. Payments are arranged monthly or quarterly for the convenience of the unit holder.

UTILITY STOCK Issue of a publicly regulated utility company. Generally, these are dividend-oriented investments since a large part of the earnings are paid to stockholders. Utility income no longer provides special tax advantages to stockholders.

YIELD The rate of return on an investment that pays out earnings. Bond yields account for three kinds of calculations.

The *coupon yield* is a fixed percentage rate by contract per $1,000 face value of the bond. If the bond was not bought at par, the current yield would be different from the coupon yield. The *current yield* is the rate of return on the dollars invested usually given at an annual percentage: annual interest return divided by current market value. The *yield to maturity* is a complex formula that accounts for both current yield and dollar differential between purchase price and maturity value. Most bonds are quoted on the basis of yield to maturity.

ZERO COUPON BOND Bonds issued at a discount to par. They make no periodic payments, although the implied rate of interest is an annually taxable event on taxable bonds. All interest is due on maturity. Market value will reflect the implied accrued interest.

ACKNOWLEDGMENTS

THE original impetus for writing this book came from a family member, recently widowed, who asked me for financial help. The outline we worked out evolved into a book with detailed explanations of how any woman can do her own financial planning and put the plan into effect. But it was the many financial seminars I have conducted that broadened my understanding of the problems women face in dealing with money. The questions asked at these seminars pointed the way. That is why this book is about why, and how, to take control of your own finances.

The stories in this book are composites of real women I have encountered in my investment brokerage practice. My intention was to retain the reality of their tales while protecting individual personalities and their privacy. By sharing these collective stories, I hope to illuminate those areas that would be most helpful to all of us.

Especially, my thanks to Joni Evans, formerly of Simon and Schuster, for her personal interest in this book, her immediate understanding of why women would need to read it, and her continuous support of this project.

I appreciate the patience and expertise of Frederic W. Hills, senior editor and vice-president at Simon and Schuster. The book would never have reached a successful conclusion without his help.

My thanks to all the women who have shared their thoughts with me. In particular, I thank the management of Neiman-Marcus of San Diego, California, for its continuing interest in women's issues.

Ellen Thro helped me in initiating the project, added creative ideas, edited, and consoled me on my concerns about writing.

John Farrish, my "democratic" brokerage manager, was my original sponsor and continuing enthusiastic supporter.

Geri Sander, an accountant, demonstrated a way to simplify tax concepts by her clear explanations at my seminars.

Many others have helped, too, and encouraged me in this enterprise. Of utmost importance, all have applauded the efforts of women to claim effective control of their lives.

INDEX

ABOUT THE AUTHORS

Anne Kohn Blau became an investment broker in 1977 in San Diego, California, after an earlier sales career in radio and television advertising in southern Florida and Mississippi. Her achievements within the financial community were recognized by her appointment as vice president of investments at Prudential-Bache Securities and subsequently at Shearson Lehman Brothers.

While writing this book, Ms. Blau continued to do financial consulting and completed an M.A., focusing on her deep concern with women's economic problems and a desire to promote their self-empowerment. In addition to her work as a financial consultant, she is a financial columnist for *Lear's* magazine.

Ellen Thro is a free-lance writer who lives and works in San Diego.